I0100363

Meaning
Matters

Essays by
David Chan

Published by

World Scientific Publishing Co. Pte. Ltd.
5 Toh Tuck Link, Singapore 596224
USA office: 27 Warren Street, Suite 401-402, Hackensack, NJ 07601
UK office: 57 Shelton Street, Covent Garden, London WC2H 9HE

British Library Cataloguing-in-Publication Data
A catalogue record for this book is available from the British Library.

MEANING MATTERS
Essays by David Chan

Copyright © 2021 by David Chan

All rights reserved.

ISBN 978-981-125-068-2 (hardcover)
ISBN 978-981-125-069-9 (ebook for institutions)
ISBN 978-981-125-070-5 (ebook for individuals)

For any available supplementary material, please visit
https://www.worldscientific.com/worldscibooks/10.1142/12680#t=suppl

Desk Editor: Sandhya Venkatesh

Typeset by Stallion Press
Email: enquiries@stallionpress.com

Meaning Matters

Essays by David Chan

David Chan

Singapore Management University, Singapore

World Scientific

NEW JERSEY · LONDON · SINGAPORE · BEIJING · SHANGHAI · HONG KONG · TAIPEI · CHENNAI · TOKYO

To all who are interested in meaning matters;
To all who believe that meaning matters; and also
To those who wonder what, why, how and when.

Here's What Fifty Leaders From Different Sectors Said About This Book …

FROM NATIONAL LEADERS

"Through his essays, Professor David Chan shows us that understanding human behaviour and attitudes is key in facing different situations and crises. In *Meaning Matters*, he offers valuable insights on how individuals, the society and the Government can strengthen our psychological defence against the COVID-19 virus as we manage the pandemic. In times of crisis, David reminds us that public trust is an invaluable asset for us to emerge stronger from this pandemic as one united nation."

Mr Gan Kim Yong
Minister for Trade and Industry, Singapore

"*Meaning Matters* brings its readers to a journey of discovery and exploration into key issues that resonate deeply with many — students, corporates, civil servants, policy makers, and politicians. It allows for self-reflection at different junctures on the meaning of "meaning" — how we make sense of the world around us, and its impact on our individual lives and our interactions with those we connect with. David's writings always spur such intense processes and yet enable the reader to emerge enlightened and inspired. He makes science so reachable and identifiable to almost everyone's lived experiences. Indeed, his writings always give meaning to our lives and this book is yet another testimony of it!"

Dr Mohamad Maliki Osman
Minister in the Prime Minister's Office,
Second Minister for Education & Foreign Affairs, Singapore

"We are a very action-oriented community, focused on problem solving. This is practically important as we try to make sure we are, as S Rajaratnam put it, a "Democracy of deeds and not words". But it is exceedingly important to always start with the "why", take a step or even a number of steps back to review, and remind ourselves of the reason and our purpose. As human beings, there is an innate need to be purposeful and be purpose-driven because everyone wants to have a personal sense of meaning and feel that they matter. David's insights are useful reminders for us to reflect, to resolve, and not just do. We live in a world that seems to be wired to respond immediately and emotionally to everything. We need to pause and think, so that we can move forward more meaningfully. David's writings do just that, and we need it more than ever before."

Mr Tan Chuan-Jin
Speaker of the Parliament of Singapore

"Professor David Chan has been a long-time observer and commentator on the state of Singapore society and issues of public interest, critically examining them through the penetrating lens of psychology and behavioural sciences. His third series of essays encapsulates the contemporary issues facing our society and offers insights on what matters most to Singaporeans, including very timely analyses of emerging issues surfaced by the COVID-19 pandemic. It offers well-considered suggestions on how we can each play a role in shaping our collective presence and future, to become more caring, confident and cohesive as a nation."

Mr Edwin Tong
Minister for Culture, Community and Youth &
Second Minister for Law, Singapore

"Professor David Chan's essays examine critical themes and issues that are relevant to the times we live in. At the heart of his writings is a firm belief that knowledge can, and should, be translated into constructive, practical applications while never losing sight of one's purpose. His insights provide food for thought for policymakers, professionals, volunteers in our social service sector, and many others who dedicate themselves to serve individuals and families in need, and to build a more caring society."

Mr Masagos Zulkifli
Minister for Social and Family Development,
Second Minister for Health &
Minister in Charge of Muslim Affairs, Singapore

FROM ACADEMIC AND UNIVERSITY LEADERS

"As a public intellectual, David Chan has made a valuable contribution to draw attention to the psychological aspects of any issue or phenomenon. He has deepened our understanding on what ails our society and how to craft solutions better. *Meaning Matters* is the third compilation of his writings and should be read."

Professor Chan Heng Chee
Professor, Lee Kuan Yew Centre for Innovative Cities,
Singapore University of Technology and Design,
Chairman, ISEAS-Yusof Ishak Institute &
Ambassador-at-Large, Ministry of Foreign Affairs,
Singapore

"Having read many of David's essays and listened to his lectures, he is certainly someone who is diverse in his interests, prolific in his expression and insightful in his thinking. On various occasions, he points us to consider an issue from the "other person's perspective" and as a result, reframe it in fresh light. In *Meaning Matters*, we are reminded once again to understand the motivation behind what people do, and on an individual level, on what matters in life. This is timely, for life is short."

Professor Cheong Koon Hean
Chairman, Centre for Liveable Cities,
Ministry of National Development, Singapore &
Chairman, Lee Kuan Yew Centre for Innovative Cities,
Singapore University of Technology and Design

"David brilliantly examined "meaning matters" in the context of how people think, feel and act as they make sense of what their experiences mean to them. Through his life experiences, David highlighted the significance of understanding the context of "meaning" in our life, which is especially crucial to maintain our individual well-being and contribute to a strong Singapore society in this era of long-term uncertainties and changes."

Professor Chong Tow Chong
President
Singapore University of Technology and Design

"You have to credit David for his ability to find the pain points in our society and come up with a set of practical proposals and solutions, which are always anchored in good science. Precisely because his approach is based on rigorous scientific insights, his analysis and suggestions are not like opinions limited to and shaped by the time of publication, but are enduring. Do I always agree with David's ideas? Not really, but he always makes me reflect and question my own beliefs. It was also interesting to re-read a few of these chapters in light of what happened in 2020 and 2021. David's insights remain valid and useful, even years after publication. Therefore, it is great to see this collection of articles bundled together. By reading them all at once, readers will start seeing the underlying common themes, and truly understand what meaning is in our Singapore society."

Professor Arnoud De Meyer
Professor Emeritus
Singapore Management University

"David Chan has produced yet another volume pulling together his opinion editorials in the local newspapers. They continue to address issues that matter, and together, serve as a convenient resource for those looking for a digestible read and common-sensical advice, written with his signature mnemonics."

Professor Lily Kong
President
Singapore Management University

"In an increasingly volatile, uncertain, complex and ambiguous world where changes are gathering pace, understanding meaning for self and others is particularly important for personal well-being, healthy interpersonal relationships, and social cohesion. Once again, drawing from his professional insights, David has exercised his gift of writing thought-provoking pieces on such critical issues in a manner that connects with the non-specialist. This collection of essays is a feast for the mind!"

Professor Ling San
Deputy President & Provost
Nanyang Technological University, Singapore

"As in his first two volumes, David has once again put together a collection of insightful essays on issues of life and living that matter to all of us. His approach to the book theme of *Meaning Matters* is fascinating. Many scholars and thinkers have written about meaning and purpose, but David's analysis provides a unique blend of scientific rigour and practical relevance that will help us deal with current issues and future challenges as we navigate new realities in a changing Singapore society. This is a must-read book."

Professor Kishore Mahbubani
Distinguished Fellow, Asia Research Institute,
National University of Singapore &
Co-author of *The ASEAN Miracle: A Catalyst For Peace*

"David Chan is Professor of Psychology. But more important he is a scholar, an intellectual, and a concerned member of the society in which we all live. The essays in this book bring together all three of these dimensions: they contemplate what scholarship and thinking reveal of how we navigate our social journey. The essays shed light on what the things around us mean — because meaning matters — and in doing so help all of us understand ourselves more deeply, and thus help each of us become better versions of ourselves."

Professor Danny Quah
Dean, Lee Kuan Yew School of Public Policy,
National University of Singapore

"Engagingly interesting and yet profoundly meaningful, this collection of 18 essays by David Chan strikes at the core of our Life's journey — what really matters. Taking himself and his own experiences, David's narratives are both very personal as well as analytically professional being a highly acclaimed academic psychologist. Through these essays, David explains what and why certain issues matter to people, and how they are dealt with across a wide assortment of these issues. He does not stop there as he shows that understanding these critical issues will greatly enable the State to design effective policies and mechanisms commensurating with people's aspirations and deep concerns, and ultimately fostering a strong, caring Singapore society. Highly illustrative in relevant examples, *Meaning Matters* is a book for everyone."

Professor Euston Quah
Director, Economic Growth Centre,
Nanyang Technological University, Singapore &
President, Economic Society of Singapore

"Professor David Chan's book, *Meaning Matters*, is the third in a collection, put together from essays written for the public. In this latest volume, Professor Chan continues his examination of contemporary society, based on his expertise and experience as a social and behavioural scientist. The issues he examined range from the outcomes of competition and meritocracy in schools and society, to leadership development, and the ongoing impact of the COVID-19 pandemic. In each instance, he has brought his trademark generosity, compassion, and the rigours of research and science, to offer perspectives which are nuanced and discerning, as well as offering gentle advice on how we can all strive to become more rounded, balanced and happier versions of ourselves."

Professor Tan Eng Chye
President
National University of Singapore

"In the midst of a global pandemic that upends our lives, everyone is looking for an anchor to look at the events unfolding. With so much information and probably more misinformation, increasingly, meaning matters. Thus, David's latest book capturing essays he has published during this period is one of those anchors that can help people better understand what is happening, and more importantly, give hope."

Professor Tan Thiam Soon
President
Singapore Institute of Technology

"*Meaning Matters* is a unique collection of incisive essays in which Professor David Chan analyses various socio-cultural and psychological issues from both scientific and applied perspectives. It is also admirable that David's essays resonate with many people of different persuasions because he is able to focus on people's perspectives as they respond to cope with the COVID-19 pandemic and life's various challenges. I strongly recommend everyone to read this interesting collection of essays which offer a variety of meanings that matters."

Dr S. Vasoo
Emeritus Professor, Department of Social Work,
National University of Singapore

FROM PUBLIC SECTOR LEADERS

"Through his essays, David helps us to make sense of what concerns the Singapore society. I also appreciate how he applies his expertise in behavioural sciences to offer practical approaches for fostering mutual understanding and overcoming differences. His latest book on "Meaning" is very timely. The speed of technological change is disrupting how we work and how we live. At the same time, the world must urgently address issues such as climate change and inequality. When the 'rules of the game' are changing, meaning and purpose matter more than ever before to guide us in our choices."

Dr Beh Swan Gin
Chairman
Economic Development Board, Singapore

"David continues to probe, sharply yet gently, on a variety of societal issues. His essays lead readers to ask "why", and to critically evaluate whether there are different ways to approach the "what" and "how". Being able to reflect and renew is paramount for any society's progress. Through his writings, David is doing his part to strengthen Singapore. Thank you, David!"

Mr Frederick Chew
CEO, Agency for Science, Technology and Research &
Chief, Public Sector Science &
Technology Policy & Plans Office,
Prime Minister's Office, Singapore

"David Chan is one of Singapore's top social and behavioural scientists. He stands out among his peers because his interests are very broad. His ability to connect his expertise to larger national and personal issues, and in accessible language, makes his essays always interesting and to savour.

His talent and passions are on full display in this latest book."

Mr Peter Ho
Chairman, Urban Redevelopment Authority &
Chairman, Social Science Research Council, Singapore

"I have known David for thirty years, seeing his work first as a police officer and subsequently as a psychologist providing professional assistance to the Singapore Police Force. Having closely followed his scholarly accomplishments, observed his public service contributions, and admired his thought leadership, I strongly recommend this book to anyone who wants to make sense of the changing challenges and complexities we face, bring about a positive difference to ourselves, and impact society meaningfully. Readers will benefit greatly from the valuable insights and perspectives because these essays not only reflect scientific objectivity and innovative ideas, they are also firmly rooted in David's grounded life experiences, social conscience, practical wisdom, constructive courage, and love for country."

Mr Khoo Boon Hui
Senior Fellow, Civil Service College,
Former Commissioner of Singapore Police Force &
Former President of INTERPOL

"David Chan writes in a practical and common-sensible way. In *Meaning Matters*, the "perspective taking" he advocates is for instance not an alien thing but appeals to the familiar ability we learn growing up from childhood to adulthood as socially connected individuals. If we would exercise this ability purposively — seeing from a counter-factual or alternative viewpoint — we would more likely find constructive ways for conflict resolution and also cultivate over time our capacity to embrace diversity and grow empathy. David always goes beyond the "what" of an issue — in discussing the "why" and "how" a situation affects us the way it does, he often also shows us what we can choose to do about it."

Mr Benny Lim
Chairman, Temasek Foundation &
Chairman, National Parks Board, Singapore

"Meaning indeed matters. Meaning founded on common values and global challenges to humanity also matters, perhaps more so, much more."

Mr Lim Chuan Poh
Chairman
Singapore Food Agency

"Professor David Chan challenges us to think of the what's, why's, and how's of life. The essays may be short, but the ideas deserve time for absorption and reflection. They cover a wide variety of topics and contexts, but every essay offers meaning to our lives. We may not agree with some of the views, but they all help us discover purpose. These are not bedtime stories but nuggets for life worth living."

Professor Lim Siong Guan
Professor, Lee Kuan Yew School of Public Policy,
National University of Singapore &
Co-author of *The Leader, The Teacher & You* and
Winning with Honour

"David Chan cogently illustrates in this collection of thoughtful essays how the *meaning* we attach to things shapes our responses. In doing so, David is once again helping us better understand ourselves as a society. This understanding of why people think and feel differently about issues is key to staying cohesive even as we become more diverse. David brings to these essays his deep scholarship, disarming candour, and heartfelt empathy, conveying profound insights with crystal clarity. This book is both an education and a delight to read."

Mr Ravi Menon
Managing Director
Monetary Authority of Singapore

"Whether one agrees or disagrees with David, he has the knack of giving a different perspective to a wide range of current issues which policymakers grapple with. He does so from the perspective of a top psychologist's point of view, grounded on empirical data and a deep understanding of the human psyche. His deep insights and analyses often help one to understand the increasing complexities of society and the difficult trade-offs policymakers have in governing."

Mr Niam Chiang Meng
Chairman, Maritime and Port Authority of Singapore &
Chairman, Mediacorp Pte. Ltd.

"In this book, Professor David Chan explores a wide range of issues around the central theme of "meaning". Written in his typical lucid and thoughtful style, the book provides many valuable and practical insights. The COVID-19 pandemic has reignited explorations about meaning and purpose, in many individuals, communities and institutions, and readers will find the book a very useful resource of ideas and concepts."

Professor Tan Chorh Chuan
Chief Health Scientist, Ministry of Health, Singapore &
Executive Director,
MOH Office for Healthcare Transformation

"David's collection of insightful essays highlights the importance of understanding meaning in our everyday living and in our everyday communication. We live in a diverse society with multi-racial, inter-generational and other group differences in attitudes and values, but as shown in David's essays, we can be a cohesive society and united community when we appreciate what it means to be committed to our country and have genuine empathy, care and concern for others."

Mrs Mildred Tan
Chairman, Singapore Totalisator Board &
Chairman, Singapore University of Social Sciences

"David's writings never fail to make me reflect on why individuals and our society act or behave in particular ways in response to the current affairs of the day. His use of layman language and easy-to-understand explanations make the articles interesting and engaging."

Mr Tan Tee How
Chairman, National Healthcare Group &
Chairman, Casino Regulatory Authority, Singapore

"David has the rare talent of a scholar who can explain complex social and psychological issues simply and clearly.

His articles are therefore always worth reading if a policy maker or layman wishes to have a conceptual framework to think about matters relevant to Singapore."

Mr Eddie Teo
Chairman
Council of Presidential Advisers, Singapore

FROM PRIVATE SECTOR LEADERS

"When leaders are making complex decisions, it is always very challenging to integrate a multitude of considerations into the decision-making process and to arrive at the most optimal one. David's collection of essays is excellent in providing a practical framework to bridging considerations as diverse as our value systems to pragmatism. I have found it very useful at both the professional and personal levels."

Mr Cheng Hsing Yao
Chief Executive Officer, GuocoLand &
Nominated Member of Parliament, Singapore

"When professors integrate science and practice to produce theoretical insights and solve real-world problems, they not only do their university proud but also serve as role models for what it means to make a meaningful impact on society. David is an example of such professors. Read and re-read these thought-provoking essays to find new ideas on meaning matters and new perspectives on what it means to make a positive difference."

Mr Ho Kwon Ping
Executive Chairman, Banyan Tree Holdings &
Chairman, Singapore Management University

"Meaning matters indeed! This collection of essays by Professor David Chan is a valuable reference toolkit for business leaders. From the search for meaning, why smart leaders fail, why people self-sabotage, to dealing and living with COVID-19, this book helps us to better understand ourselves and those we work with, and how we can be more effective."

Mr Lam Yi Young
Chief Executive Officer
Singapore Business Federation

"David's writings provide crucial insights into how Singapore can develop its social and emotional maturity. He guides us to critically examine what we really value and asks if how we think, feel and act makes sense and what it means for each of us as individuals and collectively as a society. Instead of arguing what alternative views to adopt or advocate, David provides us a frame of reference to understand purpose and priorities, and how to shift paradigms in principled and pragmatic ways."

Ms Lim Sau Hoong
Former CEO & Executive Creative Director
10AM Communications

"I have read David's columns and essays with great interest for many years. The matters he writes on always resonate for their interest in the human aspects of policy and current affairs, often giving them a relevance that extends beyond the subject matter at hand. These essays are highly accessible and condense many complex issues into material that is clear and understandable, making them richly rewarding for the reader. The depth and breadth of the material covered is quite impressive and I hope you will enjoy reading them as much as I have."

Mr Loh Lik Peng
Chief Executive Officer
Unlisted Collection: Hotels & Restaurants

"In *Meaning Matters*, David examined various issues that matter to many of us in many ways, such as taking feedback seriously, why smart leaders fail, why people self-sabotage, and the perils of excessiveness where virtue can become vice. He also devoted a series of essays on dealing with the COVID-19 pandemic, and I am particularly struck by his emphasis on positivity and building psychological capital to enhance our psychological defence. David's writings help us to reflect in ways that will contribute to our individual well-being and a strong Singapore society. Like me, I believe readers of this book will similarly resonate with the many points raised in David's essays, and perhaps, find new perspectives and meaning in many aspects of life and living in Singapore."

Mr Sim Gim Guan
Executive Director
Singapore National Employers Federation

"I have been reading David's essays and observing his other contributions as a thought leader for many years now. As mentioned to him on several occasions, I am always struck by two fascinating features of David's works and the ideas he expressed. One is the accuracy of the many future-oriented points he made, prior to significant events unfolding in

Singapore. The other is the continuous relevance of his works over time such that re-reading his essays at any time often brings about fresh insights and practical applications to the wide variety of prevailing issues. I strongly recommend reading this book now and re-reading it in the future."

Mr Gerald Singham
Global Vice Chair & ASEAN CEO,
Dentons Rodyk & Davidson LLP

"David Chan's purpose-driven writing always presents itself passionately, on issues which matter. Ultimately, the essays dissect complex issues facing Singapore and challenge the reader to think about his or her role in society. He is clear, thought-provoking and comments critically, courageously and constructively, always reasoned and reasonable. The book is a meaningful way to spend time on things which matter."

Ms Debra Soon
Group Head, Marketing & Communications,
Aviva, Singlife

"It has been said that truth is correspondence with reality and that beliefs may or may not correspond with reality. In this day and age of information overload, I find David's perspectives to be a useful reality check and very relevant in my professional and community work. This book will be a valuable resource and a precious keepsake in my collection; while I eagerly await his next essay."

Mr Tan Kian Hoon
Managing Director, Suntec Real Estate Consultants &
Chairman, National Council on Problem Gambling,
Singapore

"We grow up in an environment that often suggests there is only one right answer for important questions. David's book reminds us that sometimes there are multiple right answers that may be equally valid in different ways, which becomes clearer when we can see things from another's perspective and appreciate how the same facts can have different meanings. In his usual gifted way of explaining complex issues in simple language, David not only makes us aware of important differences but also does it in a way that unites instead of divides us. I urge everyone to read David's essays because if we really want to build an inclusive society, then it indeed matters that we understand various differences in meanings and perspectives."

Mr Stanley Tan
Chief Executive Officer, GYP Properties Limited &
Co-Founder, Asia Philanthropy Circle

"David Chan's latest book contains a number of chapters on COVID-19. COVID-19 is a challenge to human communities, bringing out the best and worst in us. Some communities are strengthened in their collective response. Others are weakened. It matters what, why, how and when decisions are made. David analyses the factors that foster positivity and counter negativity, and the psychology of trust. It is a book full of useful insights."

Mr George Yeo
Senior Advisor
Kerry Group & Kerry Logistics Network

FROM PEOPLE SECTOR LEADERS

"I am a fan of David's prolific writings on current affairs, which are rooted in the social and behavioural sciences. He explains the common and uncommon puzzles in our lives with academic rigour and logic in an engaging and practical way. His analyses and insights have informed and helped crystalise my thinking on social issues and paradigms."

Mr Willie Cheng
Chairman, Catholic Foundation &
Author of *Doing Good Well, Doing Good better* and
Doing Good Great

"Meaning does matter, particularly in this information-overload world proliferated by constant feed of inputs from internet and social media. In his latest book, which is a collection of one-and-a half dozen of snippets of a wide range of topics written over the last three years, David Chan suggested an innovative way of understanding and dealing with issues with "3Ws & 1H" — "What it means", "Why it means", "When it means" and "How it means". This approach opens up a new horizon."

Mr Chng Hwee Hong
Former Chairman
Yellow Ribbon Singapore

"David is a reflective person, and his essays reflect his deep belief in various issues. He personifies the mature modern Singaporean who takes a position on sensitive issues and dares to speak up. One need not agree partially or even entirely with his views, but his essays are a basis for constructing one's position on the subject. Reflecting on a range of issues goes a long way towards self-discovery. Pondering on David's collection of essays has assisted me in affirming my own beliefs or, at the very least, providing greater clarity."

Mr Gerard Ee
Chairman
Agency for Integrated Care, Singapore

"Everything David Chan writes helps me better understand Singapore, my fellow Singaporeans, humanity, and myself. Like a true Master (Chef), he selects the most challenging material-problem spaces, controversial topics, sensitive issues, and sacred cows, and he transforms them into something appetising, digestible, and above all, supremely nourishing. The reader is left simultaneously fully satisfied and yet craving for more. David Chan is a Singapore Brand that is Global, Local, and Personal."

Dr Geh Min
Immediate Past President, Nature Society of Singapore &
Former Nominated Member of Parliament, Singapore

"David always manages to deliver power-packed questions with a velvet glove. In this always-on, hyper-stimulated and competitive culture, it is easy to fall prey to groupthink, dominant narratives or 280 characters not out of mal-intent but as a coping mechanism. We all need to slow down, practise reflective thinking, and listen to others to more truly and deeply know the myriad of life experiences that co-exist in our nation. I hope this book creates that opportunity to slowly sip these mind-frames and explore worlds that will enrich our own for the benefit of all."

Ms Melissa Kwee
Chief Executive Officer
National Volunteer and Philanthropy Centre, Singapore

"David is like an oracle, who can be counted on for truth-telling, especially when issues are complex and hidden. We should read him — and I always do — because it helps us reflect on insights that we can easily miss while we carry out business as usual. This could either be from failure to self-reflect or from mistakes from cognitive distortions. I particularly like the essays "Why smart leaders fail" and "Why people self-sabotage", perhaps because they help me make sense of the people around us."

Mr Laurence Lien
Chairman, Lien Foundation &
Chairman, Asia Philanthropy Circle

"This collection of essays is vintage David Chan — hard hitting, calling out awkward realities and speaking truth to power, and written with the sincerity and warmth of an educator lifting up his students. A must-read for all who are finding and helping others find meaning."

Associate Professor Jeremy Lim
Chairman, Dover Park Hospice &
Director, Global Health,
Saw Swee Hock School of Public Health,
National University of Singapore

"I have always enjoyed reading David's articles as they are simply written and provide insights that sometimes resonate with me and other times give a new perspective to things that we as a society may not have thought about. Meaning does matter as it influences and shapes how we respond to issues and the perspectives we take. I am glad to see this collection of essays documented in this book as it will be a useful reference and resource for many individuals in diverse roles or with different responsibilities."

Dr Sudha Nair
Executive Director
PAVE

"Things matter to us only when it has meaning, and yet we often do not pause sufficiently to reflect on why things matter and what those meanings are to ourselves and others. In this volume of essays, David shines the light on issues that matter and translates them into valuable knowledge that contribute to our individual well-being and a strong Singapore society. By highlighting societal issues and analysing what they mean, these essays provide readers with the necessary pause for reflection and debate. A "must-read" for all who strive to live with purpose and meaning."

Dr Mary Ann Tsao
Chairperson
Tsao Foundation

Contents

About the Author

Professor David Chan received his PhD in Industrial and Organizational Psychology from Michigan State University. He is Professor of Psychology and Director of the Behavioural Sciences Initiative at the Singapore Management University (SMU) and Adjunct Principal Scientist and Scientific Advisor at the Agency for Science, Technology and Research (A*STAR) in Singapore. He is a recipient of the Lee Kuan Yew Fellowship Award for Research Excellence. He was formerly Co-Director of the Centre for Technology and Social-Behavioural Insights jointly established by A*STAR and SMU. He was also formerly Deputy Provost of SMU, Deputy Director of Wharton-SMU Research Centre, and the founding Interim Dean of the SMU School of Social Sciences.

Professor Chan's research includes areas in behavioural sciences and public policy, research methods and data analyses, longitudinal modeling, multilevel issues, personnel selection, adaptation to changes at work, and subjective well-being. His works have been published in top psychology, management, and methods journals such as *Annual*

Review of Organizational Psychology and Organizational Behavior, Applied Psychological Measurement, Cognition, Journal of Computational Social Science, Current Directions in Psychological Science, Human Performance, Intelligence, International Review of Industrial and Organizational Psychology, Journal of Applied Psychology, Journal of Personality and Social Psychology, Multivariate Behavioral Research, Organizational Behavior and Human Decision Processes, Organizational Research Methods, Personality and Social Psychology Bulletin, Personnel Psychology, Professional Psychology, and Social Indicators Research. He has authored or edited 14 books published by Routledge, SAGE, and World Scientific in various areas of social and behavioural sciences as well as on social, political and psychological issues in Singapore.

In 2000, Professor Chan was ranked 9th world-wide in the Top 100 most published researchers of the 1990's in the top journals of Industrial and Organizational Psychology. In 2020, a Stanford University global study of researcher impact named him in the top one percent worldwide among all scientists across all disciplines. Currently, his works have been cited over 13,000 times in various disciplines. He has received numerous international scholarly awards including the Dissertation Research Award from the American Psychological Association and the Scientist-Practitioner Presidential Recognition Award, the Raymond Katzell Award in Industrial and Organizational Psychology, the Distinguished Early Career Contributions Award, the Edwin Ghiselli Award for Innovative Research Design, and the William Owen Scholarly Achievement Award from the Society for Industrial and Organizational Psychology.

He has served as Senior Editor of the *Asia Pacific Journal of Management*, Associate Editor of the *Journal of Organizational Behavior*, Advisory Editor for *Oxford Bibliographies (Management)* published by the Oxford University Press, member on editorial boards of several journals and reviewer for several grant agencies in United States, Hong Kong and Singapore.

Professor Chan is consultant to numerous public, private and people sector organisations in Singapore. He currently serves as a member of the Social Science Research Council, the National Taskforce on Diabetes Prevention and Care, and the Singapore-Japan Joint Committee on Science and Technology; a director on the Board of the National Parks (NParks) Board; and Chairman of the Selection Panel for the A*STAR's Social Sciences Innovation Seed Fund. He has also previously served as a member of Public Hygiene Council, the National Council on Problem Gambling (NCPG), the International Panel of Experts and the Research and Development Advisory Panel for the Urban Redevelopment Authority, the International Advisory Panel for the SkillsFuture Singapore and the Workforce Singapore, the Governing Board for the Workplace Safety and Health Institute, the Research Advisory Panel for the National Population and Talent Division; a director on the Board of the Agri-Food and Veterinary Authority, the Board of the Singapore Corporation of Rehabilitative Enterprises, and the Board of the National Volunteer and Philanthropy Centre; and Chairman of the International Advisory Panel to the NCPG.

He is a recipient of the Long Service Volunteer Award and the Outstanding Volunteer Award from the Ministry of Social and Family Development, the Long Service Volunteer Award and the Special Recognition Honour by the Ministry of Home Affairs for outstanding contributions to the Home Team in the field of psychology, the Medallion Award for Distinguished Service from the Ministry of National Development, and the Public Administration Medal (Silver) which is a National Day Award presented by the President of the Republic of Singapore.

Professor Chan writes op-ed articles in *The Straits Times'* By Invitation Series, which is a regular newspaper column on social issues. He appears regularly on *Channel NewsAsia* current affairs television programmes and he is the consultant to the *Channel NewsAsia*'s "Social Experiment", which is a 5-part programme series that examines human behaviours and social phenomena using scientific experiments, as well as "Days of Disasters', which is an award-winning 5-part documentary series that examines the lessons learned from previous disasters in Singapore.

Together with Economics Nobel Laureate Professor Daniel Kahneman, Professor Chan served on an international committee who authored a report for the United Nations on measures of national well-being across countries that was subsequently incorporated in its UN Human Development Report. He is the first scientist in the world to receive Elected Fellow status of all six international psychological organisations namely, the American Psychological Association, the Association for Psychological Science, the International Association of Applied Psychology, the Society for Industrial and Organizational Psychology, the Society for Personality and Social Psychology and the

American Psychological Association's Division for Personality and Social Psychology.

Prior to entering academia, he was a police officer in the Singapore Police Force (SPF). In addition to serving in various operational and staff roles, he designed the SPF Assessment Centre and served as its Chief Administrator and he also assisted the SPF to conceptualize and set up its police psychological unit.

Foreword

I thank my good friend, Professor David Chan, for inviting me to contribute the foreword for this book. This is the third book of essays by him. I had also written the foreword of his first book of essays, *People Matter*.

David Chan is a rare scholar. Most scholars are trained to write for their academic peers, and they are unable to write for the general public in an effective way. David is able to write about the social and behavioural sciences in clear and simple language. He is also able to apply scientific concepts and research findings to explain many hot issues of contemporary Singapore and make practical recommendations on how to move forward. Admirably, he also writes in a non-partisan manner and dispenses wise advice to the different stakeholders, both courageously and constructively.

Take for example, his essay in Chapter 4, "Let's get the psychology of debate right". The essay examines the controversial incident in which an academic, Dr Thum Ping Tjin, was questioned for several hours by Minister K Shanmugam in the Select Committee on Deliberate Online

Falsehoods. Using the incident as a point of departure to make larger points on constructive debates, David stresses the fundamental importance of getting the facts right, accountability, intellectual honesty, mutual respect for different viewpoints, freedom to criticise and right of a robust reply. He distinguishes between harmful cynicism and healthy criticism, and advocates creating an atmosphere which "will enable us to address differences in a civil, healthy manner and move forward cohesively, even if disagreements continue to exist."

Another essay which I like very much is in Chapter 11, "Why smart leaders fail". The gist of his argument is that top academic ability is not a guarantee of success in real life. To succeed, a leader must also have the ability to judge practical situations effectively and not just behave proactively. In our subsequent conversations, I found out that this notion of situational judgment ability is an area of research and practice that David has worked on since the 1990s, in which he combined the research findings on practical, social and emotional intelligences and integrated them to develop measures of adaptability to judge and deal with practical situations. He has received various international achievement awards for his works in this area. I agree with David on the importance of situational judgment ability, and I would add that, to succeed in this multi-cultural world, a person needs cognitive, emotional and cultural intelligence. In Chapter 6, David also brings these intelligences together as he emphasises how humility, culture sensitivity, learning orientation and perspective-taking can help us to function effectively in cross-cultural and international interactions.

There are many other gems in the book. I am glad that David has put his recent essays together in this book, and I am confident that it will be as successful as the first two book collections of his essays.

Tommy Koh
Professor of Law, National University of Singapore &
Ambassador-At-Large, Ministry of Foreign Affairs,
Singapore

Preface

This book, titled *Meaning Matters*, is a collection of 18 essays that I have written for the general public in the past three years from end 2017 to early 2021, most of which first appeared in *The Straits Times*. The essays discussed a wide range of topics including the search for meaning, what it means to give, the psychology of debate and speaking up, international interactions, the varieties of liveability, when virtue becomes vice, how to take feedback seriously, subject-based banding in schools, why smart leaders fail, why people self-sabotage and issues amid COVID-19 challenges such as beating the coronavirus, making people socially responsible, dealing with negative emotions, making critical decisions, fostering positivity and building trust.

A common theme that runs through these essays may be described as "Meaning Matters". Meaning matters refer to the subject matter of the critical issues experienced by people and what it means to them, but it is also about why the way that people think, feel and act as they make sense of what their experiences mean should matter to individual well-being and societal progress in Singapore. As a whole, the collection of essays goes beyond examining what critical issues mean or matter to people, policy making and nation building, and why they do, to focus on translating the "what it means" and "why it means" to "how it means" and "when it means".

This book is the third collection of essays following the previous two books, *People Matter* and *Psychological Capital*, which consisted of essays first published in *The Straits Times* from end 2011 to early 2015 and from early 2015 to end 2017, respectively. Similar to these two previous collections, each essay in this book was written a few days before the date of its publication in *The Straits Times*. Many of the essays reflect the current affairs of the day, but the issues continue to remain relevant in public discussions and policy deliberations in the present and the future. In fact, it is useful to interpret and examine some recent and ongoing events that occurred after publication of the essays by revisiting the issues discussed, and thinking counterfactually how things could have been better so that we learn how to make things better in future. This is a main reason why I took up the suggestion from several individuals to compile this third book collection of essays to share my thoughts with more people.

On a more personal note, my focus on meaning matters in Singapore was (and still is) influenced by my life experiences. Thus, while many of the principles and approaches that I proposed in my essays have their roots in the social and behavioural sciences, they are also partly a reflection of two foundational motivations. The first is the sense-making process in the context of the issues that I care about. The second is the personal sense of meaning in adhering to a scientist-practitioner model that affects my choices of what practical issues to focus on and drives my decisions on how to speak up courageously and constructively. I share this personal note here with readers of this book to highlight one core aspect about understanding meaning for ourselves or others, which is to translate that knowledge in ways that contribute to our individual well-being and a strong Singapore society.

Finally, I am grateful for the strong and consistent support from the 50 leaders who kindly provided endorsements for this book, as well as the encouraging feedback from many others including friends and members of the public, who have read my essays over the years. Like many writers, a prime motivation for why we continue to write is that personal sense of meaning that we derive from knowing that what we write has made or can make a positive difference to our readers.

Perhaps you are currently enjoying the multiple roles in your life or navigating the challenges that come with the responsibilities in these roles. In both ways, and for now and the future, I hope you find the essays in this book useful as a springboard for self-reflections, sense-making, internal or public discussions, and individual or collective actions.

David Chan
Professor of Psychology &
Director, Behavioural Sciences Initiative,
Singapore Management University

Chapter 1

From Police Officer to Professor: A Conversation with David Chan

(This article is an invited feature interview with Professor David Chan, conducted by the Association for Psychological Science and first published in the Observer on 30 March 2018)

Q1: What specific values or knowledge did you take away from joining the Singapore Police Force more than three decades ago that you still use today as a professor, researcher, and scientist?

My time as a police officer, which spanned nine years prior to entering academia, put me in diverse practical situations as they occur in people's lives, involving people from all backgrounds in Singapore. Through these experiences, I learned the importance of fairness and trust perceptions, empathy, adaptability and situational judgment ability, all of which are distinct from formal authority, academic abilities and technical expertise.

I came to appreciate how important it is to be sensitive to contextual factors and see things from another's perspective, to handle practical situations in a principled and pragmatic way, and to respect people's dignity. I also learned that one can use different types of power effectively and use opportunities efficaciously to make a positive difference to people's lives.

All of these experiences significantly affected my judgment and decision-making in terms of what issues to focus on and how to approach them. It could be choosing a research topic, mentoring a student or junior faculty, working with experts from diverse disciplines and different cultures, advising the government or an organisation on a policy or programme, consulting for a television documentary series, writing an op-ed for a newspaper, or volunteering for a cause.

Q2: One of your current lines of research focuses on perspective-taking. Why has that received much attention from policymakers and the public?

Studies have shown that we don't see things as they are; we see things as we are. We make interpretations according to our beliefs and past experiences, and also in context of the circumstances we find ourselves in. We need to recognize that some of the differences in viewpoints across individuals or groups, or between citizens and policymakers, are probably due, in part, to differences in life experiences. We cannot live someone else's life experiences. But if we all take time to put ourselves in someone else's shoes before we advocate a position or react to differing views, it is more likely that we can move forward constructively, even if disagreements still occur.

So, I think the attention that my work received is quite natural, in the sense that disagreements are not uncommon and they are often unpleasant. Perspective-taking offers an adaptive approach to solving problems and making decisions in the real world.

Q3: Are there specific strategies we can use to activate perspective-taking when talking to someone who is different from us?

There are evidence-based approaches to enhance our perspective-taking abilities and tendencies in an adaptive way — for example, guarding against our confirmatory biases by learning to be inclusive and to honestly consider other perspectives very different from our own.

But don't just imagine possible perspectives in an armchair. Get into the action and interact with others to find out their concerns and circumstances. When these interactions are naturalistic as opposed to contrived, people are more likely to tell each other what they truly think instead of what they think the other wants to hear. Over time, quality interactions build mutual trust, reciprocity norms, social cohesion, and possibly even shared values on some core issues. All these will motivate people to see things from each other's perspective and facilitate conflict resolution and collaboration.

Q4: Based on your experiences as a scientist, professor, consultant and public intellectual, what are some lessons you think would benefit students and early-career researchers?

Psychological science has so much to contribute to solving real-world problems and improving people's lives. When we learn how to address apparent contradictions and when to move away from a zero-sum, trade-offs mindset, we will see many commonalities and complementarities in goals between science and practice.

Two points are worth reiterating — they are often preached but seldom practiced. Firstly, our research can solve real problems and improve people's lives when they based on scientific rigour and practical relevance. Rigour and relevance are not merely abstract values that we profess; they are operating principles to guide actual decisions in the research process and in the communication and application of the findings. Secondly, the translation from scientific knowledge to practical applications is critical. As psychologists, we will have much practical impact if we develop the skills to effectively integrate science and practice.

Chapter 2

The Search for Meaning Amid Tasks Galore and Race to be First

In a merit-based and achievement-oriented society like Singapore, to succeed in school or at work often means standing out in a crowd and ranking ahead of other competitors. The most common performance indicators of success are tangible ones, defined by societal and group norms.

So, for students and their parents, academic scientists and professors, and people in various occupations and organisations, concrete outcomes like academic grades, journal publications and awards, income and wealth, or promotion and power have become the widely accepted ladder of success that drives what they do, and how they do it.

But the pursuit of success is maladaptive when the competitive comparison with others and the craving for salience dominate how we think and feel, and what we do. It will constantly produce stress and strain at the various stages and moments of our lives. It is easy to end up forgetting why we engaged in an endeavour, joined a community or a cause, or even chose an occupation or organisation in the first place.

SCIENCE AND MEANING

Take, for example, the role of academic scientists and their reason for doing science. In a science feature interview published two weeks ago in The Straits Times, I said: "Why are we doing science? It has to be because we want to solve human problems and enhance human well-being. It cannot be to publish in top journals and win awards. That should be the consequence of good science, not the reason for doing it."

Not surprisingly, I received many responses from academics and users of science including policymakers and leaders of public-sector agencies. These individuals reacted positively because they believe in translational research and evidence-based practice — the need to apply scientific research to address practical issues. They know that good science solves real problems.

But somewhat unexpected was the responses received from those who are not academics, scientists or direct users of scientific findings. They shared with me the things they put effort in and spend their time on, and how they are motivated by the personal meaning they find in doing what they believe in, and care about. Most involve contributing to society and making a positive difference to the lives of others in various ways.

A common theme in the comments of many of these Singaporeans from all walks of life was that their personal sense of meaning and well-being came about after they realised how overly consumed they had been in pursuing a singular dimension of success. These dimensions had to do with academic grades in school, a promotion or political power at work, or more wealth and fame — relative to what others had.

MATTERS OF THE MOMENT

Zero-sum competition and comparison with others can lead to adverse consequences, for self and others. Here are some examples — egocentric thoughts lacking in empathy; negative emotions such as anxiety and anger; social divides that breed elitism, envy, contempt and conflict; and selfish acts that advance oneself at the expense of others. These consequences make it difficult to build interpersonal trust and good quality social relationships, which are among the strongest predictors of individual well-being, group morale and group cohesion.

But beyond these more obvious consequences, there are silent effects that creep into our daily routines and influence how we think, feel, and behave. They proceed quickly, moment by moment, resulting in a negative spiral that becomes harder to stop over time. Here are some danger signs that we may have "normalised" in our daily lives:

- Undiscerning. Concerned with competition from others, an individual takes on every task assigned or available. He works tirelessly to complete them, often providing more details than necessary and without regard to the distribution of work among co-workers.
- Need to win. Fixated on proving one's superiority, an individual is out to win a debate or argument at all

cost — never mind the feelings of others and the adverse effect of his responses on them.

- Risk avoidance. Worried about looking bad relative to others, an individual avoids having to do something new or that might lead to him failing or appearing incompetent. This ends up in missed opportunities, errors of omission, and good advice rendered ineffective due to delayed adoption.

The individual caught in a negative spiral of maladaptive performance could be any one of us. At stake is our physical, mental and social health.

Maladaptive performance episodes, which are momentary threats to our well-being, are mutually and self-reinforcing and thus make up a negative spiral. But we are unaware of the danger because each threat appears as a small and necessary daily burden that we take as a given that we have to bear or live with.

It is like being the victim of an abusive or exploitative close relationship. If we are unable or unwilling to identify the danger signs, take action early and react adaptively, it becomes more difficult to get out of the spiral. We could end up like the metaphoric frog that was slowly boiled alive.

WHAT REALLY MATTERS

The dangers of maladaptive performance goals can be countered with mastery and learning goals. The latter shift one's focus to mastering deep skills in a task domain, instead of trying to outdo everyone in every task. They also encourage a genuine learning orientation that seeks to understand issues, contexts and people.

Research has also identified the job characteristics that help make work meaningful. For example, it is enriching to perform tasks that are complex enough to be challenging but achievable, based on one's competence. We also want some autonomy or control over how to carry out and accomplish the task activities; and we want useful feedback on how we are performing.

Work is also more meaningful when there is a good fit between the person's profile of abilities and needs and what the work demands and offers.

Learning and mastery goals, job characteristics and person-work fit are all important for meaningful work. I call them "process meaning" because they are all about how we do the work. But there is also an equally important aspect of what makes work meaningful, which I call "outcome meaning". This is about why we do what we do, and the impact of what we do.

Outcome meaning is most powerful when it is other-centric, as opposed to centred on oneself. Research has shown that, across many demographics and cultures, people find their lives (and what they do) most meaningful — and they experience good well-being — when they know that they have made a positive difference to other people's lives.

Paradoxically, we achieve personal fulfilment not by putting others down, but uplifting them. Not by comparing ourselves with others, but comparing how others are better off now than before because of what we did. Put in another way, the egocentric pursuit is replaced by a people-centric approach. An approach characterised by passion and purpose, with a genuine desire to enhance the well-being of others, and not a hidden agenda for political gain or to achieve some self-interested goals.

Here is a simple self-test. Are we seeking feedback and finding out other people's needs, concerns, aspirations and viewpoints because we really want to, and not just because we have to?

MAKING A DIFFERENCE

Not every matter that we have to deal with truly matters. Of course, it is unrealistic to expect the two to always coincide. But we should distinguish what really matters from matters of the moment.

It is easy to be absorbed in the tasks and matters that require us to work hard to complete, and often to compete. But the outcome of the accomplishment may have little to do with what truly motivates us when we find meaning in doing what really matters. This is important to remember and reflect, especially when we can choose what to devote our time and life to.

Back to the reason for doing science. I asked my academic colleagues and PhD students this question, "When you die, do you want to have beside you a heap of your publications read by a select group of academics, or the peace of mind knowing that your work made a difference to the lives of many?"

The basic issue in this question is relevant to not just academics. We can replace the heap of publications with stacks of cash or collections of symbols of wealth, power and fame. Or anything we accumulated from years of stressful relentless pursuit, driven by a fixation on popular success, prestige and possession, instead of a focus on personal meaning, purpose and passion.

Life is a busy pursuit for most, and a stressful one for many. But life is short and fragile for all. Now and then, we should ask ourselves why we do what we do, and what really matters to us. To pause, remind and reflect, and maybe retrack and redirect.

Competition and comparison are not inherently unhealthy, but it is easy to slip into a negative spiral when we ignore the danger signs.

It is human to want to achieve and accomplish something significant. How then to have a sustained and sustainable sense of personal fulfilment?

Research evidence and anecdotal experiences have provided the answer: when the significance is less about salience in comparison with peers or standing out from them, and more about the positive difference that one makes to other people and the larger community that one is a part of.

Chapter 3

What it Means to Give

Earlier last week, I delivered the keynote address at a forum titled Giving Matters, organised by the National Volunteer and Philanthropy Centre.

The cross-sector event brought together more than 300 individuals from government, corporates, social enterprises and non-profit organisations to share their experiences and ideas about giving, which includes volunteering and donating.

After my speech, some participants shared with me why and how they give as well as their personal experiences in interacting with givers and recipients. Many had mixed feelings and unresolved questions. Is giving rational or emotional? Should we remind people to count their blessings to encourage them to give? How do we motivate volunteers?

I hope this essay on the psychology of giving will help shed light on the issues raised. As we reflect on what giving means to us personally, the hope is that we are inspired to do more and encourage others as well.

GENUINE GIVING AND RATIONALITY

We sometimes hear people say they want to volunteer or donate but they do not have enough time or money. Yet, across different socio-economic backgrounds, there are people who give a lot of their time, effort or money, and they do so quietly without any tangible rewards or recognition. Clearly, humans are not purely economic beings who spend their lives calculating gains and losses to arrive at decisions.

If you believe humans are homo economicus, then you will find this even more puzzling — studies show that we feel good when we give, and better when we give away something precious to us than something we have plenty of or do not need. Behavioural sciences tell us that this is not irrational, the motivation and decision to give genuinely reflect a core aspect of human rationality.

We are rational when we do things that we believe will help us progress from the status quo to reach our goal. That goal, however, need not be about material possessions or power or fame. When our goals are about lived experiences involving personal meaning, purpose and passion, our behaviours directed towards our goals are sustained, sustainable and satisfying.

Since genuine giving is unconditional, would it not result in a loss situation and so produce negative emotions for the giver?

On the contrary, studies consistently show that genuine acts of giving are associated with better physical, mental, emotional and social well-being. The benefits to well-being are long-term. There is positive impact on health and lifespans, even after taking into account other factors known to lower risk of mortality such as genetics, physiology, exercise, diet and wealth.

These results are not affected by demographics, such as sex, age, race, religion, nationality, or background like education, occupation, income and retirement status.

Givers themselves also attribute their better well-being to their acts of giving. What this means is the giver's experiences and causal beliefs create a self-reinforcing process that sustains their giving behaviours. In short, genuine giving is rational and it involves positive emotions. There is no contradiction. Not only that, rationality and emotions also complement each other to motivate people to continue giving.

THE 4Gs OF GIVING

We see both rationality and emotions at work in our own experiences of giving in Singapore. These can be looked at via what I call the 4Gs of giving — goodness, generosity, governance and gratitude.

Goodness

In parenting, and also education in schools, we try to inculcate the value of giving as a good thing in itself. Not just volunteering and donating but also the simple idea of giving or sharing with others what we have without expecting to receive something in return.

Generosity

Generous giving impresses because it goes beyond what is predicted or expected. It receives much publicity when the absolute amount given is large. Million-dollar donations or hundreds of volunteer hours by an individual are praise-worthy and newsworthy. But generous giving is most inspiring when the amount is large relative to what the giver had. It is breathtaking to see someone, especially a low-income individual, donating a substantial proportion of his money.

Another inspirational situation is when the giver chooses to be anonymous — the act is clearly about benefiting the recipient, not the donor through praise or public recognition.

Governance

We are more likely to give if we know what happens to what we give, and the way it is used fits well with why we give. So for giving to be sustainable, good governance in the charity and volunteer sectors is critical. Transparency and accountability are the key governance features that affect public trust in these intermediary organisations.

That is why it is important to have laws, regulations and codes of practice to enhance good governance in the giving sectors. They must be effective to deter, detect and deal decisively with mismanagement and wrongdoings. They must also be practical, so that they do not escalate compliance costs and create unnecessary rules that demotivate the intermediaries and stifle giving.

Gratitude

When we are grateful for our situation (count our blessings), we are more likely to engage in volunteerism and philanthropy. The converse is also true. When we help others, we become more grateful for our own life conditions as we appreciate the situation of those who are less fortunate. We will also gripe less about our life and thus experience fewer negative emotions. Gratitude and giving influence and reinforce each other. Should we then make people feel grateful so that they give to those in need?

Educators and leaders in politics, public service, and non-profit sector often try to evoke gratitude in people to nudge them to contribute to society. They highlight how much we have all personally benefited from the community and so should aim to give back to it.

Moral obligation and a sense of duty to member of one's group (organisation, community, country) make up what psychologists call normative commitment. This "ought to" commitment increases when we feel proud of the group to which we belong and identify strongly with it.

Normative commitment can evolve over time. But gratitude can neither be demanded nor requested. The gratitude message from educators and leaders works well if it is consistent with the quality of our actual lived experiences. And if we see the educators, leaders or other messengers themselves practising what they preach. To lead in changes to become a giving nation and caring society, leaders need to be role models in genuine giving.

Rather than constantly dropping heavy hints about the need to give back to society, it may be better to set up ways and means that will make it easier for people to extend help to others. The sense of well-being that comes from doing so is more likely to sustain the act of giving in the longer term.

Important as they are, the 4Gs are not all that matters. We need to move beyond them because there is much more to giving. Or, more accurately, the 4Gs truly matter only when they are focused on the positive impact on people's lives.

WHY GIVING MATTERS

Four positive people-centric outcomes make clear why giving matters.

First, giving benefits those in need and can transform their lives. A caring society must not neglect the needs of the poor and persons with disabilities. There are also other vulnerable groups, especially children, youth and elderly in dysfunctional families with problems that are multifaceted and inter-related. It may not be obvious, but their unmet needs are urgent because one problem rapidly leads to many others.

The most impactful giving is not handouts. It is giving that helps the vulnerable address the root cause of their problems, and acquire work and life skills that build and sustain their self-efficacy to solve problems, self-esteem from solving them, and self-reliance to face the future.

Second, giving can produce positive outcomes for the giver. Many studies have shown that people who volunteer or donate are more likely to be satisfied and happy with their lives. This relationship between giving and subjective well-being is robust and it remains even when controlling for income status and other background variables.

Third, giving can build and strengthen a strong organisation. When employees give through meaningful corporate social responsibility programmes, it does not just increase the organisation's public reputation and attractiveness, it also produces positive attitudes in individual employees, builds team cohesion, and contributes to organisational commitment.

Finally, giving is critical for a strong society. When people give and care for one another, the community develops social networks with interpersonal trust and reciprocity norms. This builds social capital. Both givers and recipients develop self-efficacy, become optimistic, possess hope, and become more resilient. This builds psychological capital.

Social capital and psychological capital are necessary resources to develop a strong Singapore society of adaptive individuals and communities. They contribute to the nation's total defence, with people and communities cohering when faced with national security threats and in times of health, economic, social or political crises.

In sum, the simple act of giving is more complex than we think. But however complicated the threads that bind the giver, the recipient and society, the tapestry it creates is indeed a many-splendoured thing — especially if we understand how it works.

Chapter 4

Let's Get the Psychology of Debate Right

In the last few weeks, many Singaporeans have been exercised over the lengthy debate that ensued between an academic and a government minister during a parliamentary committee hearing.

Singaporean historian Thum Ping Tjin had made a written submission to the Select Committee on Deliberate Online Falsehoods in which he asserted that the biggest purveyor of fake news in Singapore was the Government, in particular the late founding prime minister Lee Kuan Yew.

When he appeared before it to flesh out his submission, he was questioned for over six hours by Home Affairs and Law Minister K. Shanmugam, a member of the committee, over his interpretation of historical events such as the 1963 Operation Coldstore exercise.

The intense debate drew much public attention, with some feeling Dr Thum had been disrespected, and had his academic credentials torn to shreds by Mr Shanmugam. A group of more than 200 academics signed an open letter to defend him and voice their concerns.

Government leaders, meanwhile, said keeping quiet about such serious allegations was not an option and they had to debunk Dr Thum's assertion that Mr Lee "was the biggest creator of fake news in Singapore, a liar, and Operation Coldstore was based on falsehoods", as Mr Shanmugam put it.

The whole debate over truth, tact, and the treatment of Dr Thum has sadly produced much negative perception of Singapore and its Government from some observers, in and outside of Singapore.

It is not just academics who are concerned about what the episode says about the way critical debate is held in Singapore. Civil society advocates, journalists, community leaders and citizens who want to make critical comments on important issues in Singapore, are also concerned.

AN ACADEMIC'S RESPONSE

How is an academic familiar with academic values and the Singapore context, like myself, expected to respond to the issue?

First, I want to stress the fundamental point that facts do matter. Facts are empirical data that provide the information for policymakers and public to make assessments and decisions about policy and public actions. When one intentionally ignores relevant data or does not share them, it is not a confirmatory bias but an integrity issue.

Second, intellectual honesty is important. We should pursue accountability, but that does not mean it is acceptable to make unfounded allegations or forego intellectual honesty. We should be firm and fair about positions and issues, but also respect others when they hold different views even if we think they are invalid.

Third, academics and the Government both have important roles in society, and there must be mutual respect between both parties. Society must maintain the freedom for academics and other concerned citizens to express critical comments on public issues. The Government, too, has the right, and indeed responsibility, to engage those views and respond robustly where necessary. Both the freedom to criticise and the right of a robust reply are important for good governance and a problem-solving democracy. Both must not be trivialised or abused.

Good academics do not shun scrutiny of their claims, and they do not rule out the possibility that they might be wrong. Empirical disciplines emphasise openness and objectivity to scrutinise and test competing theories using data. Good academics respect facts. And they change their prior position or conclusion in the light of clear contrary evidence.

Academics who want to make a positive difference in people's lives would not only allow but want non-academics, including policymakers, to read what they write and examine their conclusions and recommendations. But they expect fair and cordial treatment in the review and interaction, especially if they see the context as a consultation or feedback-giving session.

So, we need to be clear what the academic community's issue for the Thum case ought to be. The issue is not whether Dr Thum's claims about Operation Coldstore can be questioned by non-academics in a Select Committee hearing. They can be questioned and examined, and should be, especially when they were made in a formal submission to the Select Committee, but even if the allegations were made in an academic outlet.

What matters is how the questioning was carried out in the Committee hearing, which was meant to be both a public consultation and an evidence-gathering effort. Given the interrogative and cross-examination style of questioning, it is natural for observers to be concerned, and we can debate what impact the whole Shanmugam-Thum exchange will have on academics' public comment in future.

FRAMEWORK FOR CRITICAL COMMENTS

What impact could this episode have on public debate, especially on the propensity of fellow academics to offer constructive, critical comment in future? We need to learn from the Shanmugan-Thum debate and understand the underlying psychology of critical comments so that we can have effective public discourse and public engagement.

How can one engage in debate and make critical comments in a constructive and fair manner that will allow one's views to be received and heard? I would like to propose a framework to encourage such interactions.

THE FIVE Cs

When engaging in critical comments in an interaction, we can consider the five Cs.

Competence

First is competence of the person. A critical comment is more credible when made by someone competent.

Competence refers to the knowledge and skills relevant to the issues at hand.

Formal qualifications and job titles such as university professor or a cabinet minister are proxy indicators of relevant competence. But whether a comment is valid or not depends on the factual basis and soundness of the argument.

Character

Second is character. In principle, an individual's character is separate from the validity of his argument. Which is why there is a fallacious counter-strategy called ad hominem. This approach avoids genuine discussion of the topic by attacking an individual's character traits and detracting attention from the substantive issues.

In practice though, sometimes it is necessary to consider character. If someone is deceitful or there is clear intent to cover up facts, mislead the public or sow discord, then it is legitimate to bring up character issues when engaging in critical debates, to prevent an invidious erosion of public trust and cohesion from calculated moves by manipulative characters. Where there is evidence that character is an issue, it should be brought up explicitly, and not via innuendo or through vague accusations that come across like unsubstantiated character attacks.

Courage

The third C is courage. Speak up courageously. This does not mean being uninhibited in explicating whatever happens to be in one's mind. That is impulsivity, maladaptive forthrightness, or poor situational judgment ability.

Commenting courageously means offering analyses and inferences in a way that is factual, objective, and scientifically defensible. It means speaking the truth, while aware of the potential cost, which could involve unhappiness and retaliatory actions from either the authorities or the public.

Constructive

Fourth, be constructive. To comment constructively is not about pleasing particular individuals or groups. That is impression management, populism or political correctness.

Commenting constructively means examining and explaining things that matter so that concrete solutions to problems can be co-created and practically adopted. Being constructive also means putting in the effort to make sure the critical comment is not misconstrued; and being mindful of what is said or how it is said so that the critical comment is more likely to be well-received and considered seriously.

The first four Cs — competence, character, courage and being constructive — are all attributes of a person. Someone who wants to engage better in a critical debate has a better chance of doing so effectively and being well-received when he or she possesses and practices these traits. But beyond personal attributes, the larger environment matters a great deal in terms of how supportive we are as a society in encouraging critical debate.

Climate

The fifth C is thus climate of support. People are more likely to offer courageous and constructive comments on issues when there is a socio-political climate that supports them. So we should be asking — why do commentators speak up, or decide to give up, and what kind of climate for commenting are we cultivating in Singapore?

These crucial questions deserve specific and explicit answers. It is not sufficient to make general assertions that the climate in Singapore encourages or discourages critical comments.

To get clearer answers, interact with local and foreign academics currently working in Singapore, and also concerned others such as civil society advocates, journalists and community leaders. Find out their actual experiences and expectations. Among these responses, some will reflect Singapore's reality better than others. But all responses are relevant because people's perceptions are their subjective reality, which in turn influence their attitudes and actions.

To identify and answer questions on climate, seek information on any concrete events and evidence regarding actions taken against someone for making critical comments.

More importantly, address issues of mutual trust in benevolence between academics and Government. This is about one's belief that the other will mean what it says and say what it means.

It will be most unfortunate if only negatives, and no positives, can come out of the ongoing public debate over critical comments. The worst thing that can happen is if we let ourselves be driven by a harmful cynicism, consumed by conspiratory beliefs, choosing to pick out arguments that confirm our biases, and engage in other counter-productive behaviours. Then a negative spiral of self-defeating attitudes and actions may result in our society.

An alternative way is possible, based on the 5Cs of having competence, maintaining good character, being courageous and constructive and fostering a climate supportive of healthy criticism. Such a climate can be reasonably sceptical, but must be guided by intellectual honesty, humility and practical intelligence. This will enable us to address differences in a civil, healthy manner and move forward cohesively, even if disagreements continue to exist. This is essential not just for the parties involved in the arguments, but also the many others observing and making conclusions.

Whether we are academics, journalists, policymakers, civil society advocates, community leaders or concerned citizens, there will be situations where we have to make critical comments or respond to such comments. Focusing on the five Cs will help reduce negativity, produce positivity, and co-create solutions.

We will all be better off if we get the psychology of debate right, not just the politics.

Chapter 5

Stop Calling Those Who Speak Up a 'Vocal Minority'

Government leaders in Singapore receive a lot of advice and feedback from diverse individuals and groups, both publicly and behind closed doors. Not surprisingly, there are different opinions on how appropriate leaders' reactions are and how effective their responses may be.

For several years now, there have been calls for government leaders to see things from the people's perspectives. Commentators and activists have often asked the Government to be able and willing to listen to alternative viewpoints and consider them seriously. Thus, it was not a new message this week when Members of Parliament from all sides spoke on the need for leaders to effectively engage the people and earn public trust.

Both in and outside Parliament, this point on the importance of public engagement has become more salient after last week's unexpected change of Government in neighbouring Malaysia, when the ruling coalition, which had governed for six decades, lost the general election to the opposition. Singaporeans watching across the Causeway felt as though the political tsunami that knocked the government out of power up north, was lapping at our shores. This psychological salience is not a bad thing for Singapore. It guards against complacency and reminds all to never take public trust and public engagement for granted.

REACTING TO CONTRARY VIEWS

Policymakers and governments able to take on board seriously the views from well-intentioned people will often find that such inputs contribute positively to the policy or issue at hand. This is because genuine views are relevant considerations, even if leaders disagree with them.

But the outcome will be negative if leaders react inappropriately and dismiss the contrary views without engagement. It gets worse if they attach a label with negative connotations, for example dismissing views as representing "a vocal minority". People will get upset and disengage, thus depriving the leaders of potential valuable inputs.

Emotional contagion occurs as people share with each other their negative experiences and emotions. This mutual reinforcement leads to a negative spiral. Differences in viewpoints between people and the leaders are accentuated, facts get ignored, and people seek out information to support their negative beliefs of the leaders. In some cases, people will either take flight from the leaders or fight them.

This negative scenario can occur even when leaders are neither ignorant nor arrogant, although being so will certainly contribute to it. The tendency to resist contrary views is part of our human psychology. It can apply to every leader regardless of educational background, socio-economic status, political belief and moral position.

But if leaders understand the underlying psychology, they will be not just principled but also adaptive — able to handle disagreements effectively and create a lot of good from contrary views.

VOCAL MINORITY VERSUS SILENT MAJORITY

One important psychological issue concerns using "vocal minority" and "silent majority" to describe segments of the population.

Last Sunday, Opinion editor Chua Mui Hoong wrote a commentary in The Sunday Times on five takeaways for Singapore from the Malaysian General Election. As her first takeaway, she cited a point I have often made in presentations and in my writings — about how each of us may be part of a "vocal minority" on some issue; but that the various vocal minorities can add up to a sizeable vocal majority. She concluded: "Politicians dismiss vocal minority issues at their own peril."

Put another way, there are actually many people who are voicing concerns, or trying to, in various ways, and on various issues, that matter to them. Add them up and the number can form a majority.

It also means we should not assume there is always a large silent majority who do not speak up on issues, and are somewhat happy, agreeable and share a similar view on the status quo. The size of such a silent and singular group, if it exists, is not as large as the term tends to imply.

Using the labels vocal minority and silent majority produces many other problems.

First, labelling groups does not help policymaking. Even if there is indeed a vocal minority and a silent majority on one particular policy issue and the two groups have opposing views, it does not mean that the minority is wrong, or that the majority is right.

Adaptive leaders know that positive policy changes can come from a good idea that started as a lone voice or minority viewpoint. They also know that minority views may serve to check against complacency and groupthink.

The point is this: What a position says, how valid an argument is, and how effective a policy is, are all separate from how vocal a minority is, how small or big the minority and majority groups, and what the majority wants. Group labels are not views.

Second, having a binary division of how people respond to an issue is not constructive and can have negative consequences.

Let's say you classify people into one of two mutually exclusive groups with opposing views — one a vocal minority dominating the discourse and the other a silent majority choosing not to contribute to it.

What will be the impact? It divides rather than unites people. It creates a "us-versus-them" mindset. This exclusive mindset can evolve or erupt into social divides. Some may ask the divisive question: "Are you with us or against us?"

Dividing people into two camps will not help identify what is common despite the differences, and how the differences can in fact work in complementary ways.

The binary distinction often misrepresents reality. For most major public issues such as immigration, taxes, minimum wage, and internet regulation, it is not true that there are only two different and opposing views in the population. The more complex an issue gets over time in public discourse, like that on social inequality, the greater the spectrum of views. Some people may even move their position along the spectrum.

People who are vocal can have very different views. This is clear when there are many viewpoints and disagreements in public discourse. Also, some may speak up on one aspect of a policy but others may do so on another aspect or the underlying rationale.

Those who are silent can also have very different views. But we may not know what these views are, and thus how they are similar to or different from those expressed by vocal people. Without evidence, there is no basis to say that the large group labelled as silent majority share the same view, and that it is opposite to that articulated by the vocal minority group.

ENGAGING THOSE WHO DISAGREE AND THE AMBIVALENT

Rather than dismissing those who speak up on a topic as belonging to a "vocal minority", leaders should pay more attention to those who disagree and those who are ambivalent. They span across all demographics and socio-economic classes.

People who disagree strongly with the leader on an issue may or may not speak up. For those who don't, they may express their disagreement in other ways — at the ballot box, sharing views with and influencing family, friends and colleagues in private conversations, even leaving the country. For those who speak up, they are the ones most likely to be labelled as a vocal minority.

Why engage people who disagree strongly? If they are right, it helps solve problems. If they are wrong, convince them or get them involved in a way that will help rather than hurt the situation. In many situations, it is not a given that leaders are right or wrong, so honest engagement for co-solutions is important.

Of course, groups with ulterior motives to sow discord will require leaders to take a different approach. But such groups are the exception.

The large majority of Singaporeans who speak up strongly in disagreement do so despite the costs and potential risks because they hope to make a positive difference. Calling them troublemakers or vocal minorities who cause social disharmony is not just inaccurate but also self-defeating. It will only lead them towards maladaptive and aggressive behaviours because they cannot see alternative means of engagement.

Then there are people with ambivalent views. They may have mixed feelings and conflicting thoughts. They can see the two contrasting positions each with pluses and minuses, and they are unsure what to feel, think or do about it. They are neither neutral nor indifferent.

There are probably many Singaporeans who are ambivalent about something, be it about the Government, the public sector, the opposition, a policy or a social issue. These are views that involve both positives and negatives. Ambivalence is a discomforting psychological state. The motivation to get out of it to take a position can make them more susceptible to emotion-based influences and cognitive biases.

It is not easy to effectively engage those who disagree or are ambivalent. But there is much to lose when they are not engaged.

LEADERSHIP IN ENGAGEMENT

What does all this mean for leaders? Put simply, they should not label people as belonging to a "vocal minority" when tackling a difficult issue. And do not label the rest as silent majority and assume that they agree with the issue.

Calling people a vocal minority or a silent majority hurts more than helps policymaking, social cohesion and co-creation of solutions. If we all learn to stop labelling people, initially mild or resolvable disagreements are less likely to end up in a polarisation of attitudes.

But leaders are human too. The challenge for principled leaders is to be aware of their confirmatory biases to see only the strengths in their own position and only the weaknesses in the opposing view. Being principled involves doing what one believes is the right thing, but it does not mean one is right all the time.

Principled leaders are also adaptive when they are self-aware, humble, able and willing to acknowledge mistakes and learn from them, and can see things from another's perspective.

Chapter 6

A Different Perspective:
10 Questions for David Chan

(This article is an invited feature interview with Professor David Chan, conducted by the Singapore International Foundation and first published in the 2018 Issue 2 of the Singapore Magazine)

Q1: How important is it for Singapore to build strong international relations with other countries?

As a small nation, there are two principles of pragmatism that are critical for Singapore to survive and thrive. One is upholding the international rule of law. The other is building strong international relations, trust and friendships at all levels and across all sectors. This cross-country and cross-cultural relationship building is not just between governments, but also between individuals, groups and organisations.

Q2: How do you think psychology contributes to building stronger ties with the global community?

Psychology is the science of how people think, feel and act in different situations and contexts, including various individual, interpersonal, team and cultural settings. If we understand these differences and apply it in practice, we will function more effectively in our international interactions. This is especially important in trying to build trust and relationships when there are differences in goals, interests and even values.

Q3: Is the ability to embrace different perspectives fundamental to enhancing international ties?

To enhance ties, we need to build trust and quality relationships with others, and the first step is to understand what others are thinking and to see things from their perspective. But studies have shown that we tend to be very poor at perspective-taking. In fact, we don't even see things as they are; we see things as we are. We make interpretations of ourselves and others according to our beliefs and past experiences, and also in context of the circumstances we live or find ourselves in.

We need to recognise that some of the differences in viewpoints between Singaporeans and foreigners are probably due in part to the differences in life experiences. We should take some time to put ourselves in their shoes before we advocate a position or react to differing views. It will increase the likelihood that we move forward constructively, even if disagreements still occur.

Q4: Given the current geo-political climate, why is it more important than ever to tread carefully in the areas of dispute resolution?

The current geo-political climate makes conflicts more complicated because we can no longer assume that all parties will always adhere to the international rule of law during the resolution process. It therefore becomes even more important to build relationships with trust, goodwill and reciprocity norms.

Upholding international rule of law and building relationships are not mutually exclusive. Treading carefully means making clear where we stand on issues. Our positions must be principled ones. What we decide, and how we approach issues, must also be guided by situational awareness and practical intelligence, so that our proactive behaviours lead to positive outcomes.

Q5: What does global citizenship mean to you?

There are three equally important aspects to it. The first is about having some basic knowledge or awareness of the developments outside one's country. As global citizens, we should be interested in and informed about regional and global issues. These could be specific issues such as denuclearisation in North Korea, territorial disputes concerning the South China Sea, and trade wars between countries. Or they could be larger questions about issues such as poverty and wealth disparity.

The second aspect is to be culturally sensitive to the thoughts, feelings and actions of others who are different from us. It also involves being self-aware of one's own cultural biases.

Cultural sensitivity is about understanding what the differences are, why they exist, and how to manage them in cross-cultural interaction. The differences can work to our advantage when diverse cultures complement one another.

In this way, cultural sensitivity can help to prevent bad outcomes and promote good ones.

The third aspect is to go beyond differences to focus on commonalities. To be a global citizen is to be human — to recognise that amid cultural differences and diversity, we all belong to the same human race. This involves respecting human dignity and rights, as well as caring for and helping each other, regardless of geography, passports and skin colour. It also means recognising that we share the same planet that we inhabit, and with it the responsibility to do our part to protect the environment.

Q6: Why is it important for Singaporeans to have a more global outlook and engage with communities outside the country?

The Singapore economy is highly dependent on what happens globally. Our businesses need to internationalise, and good relationships with communities outside the country require quality interactions and engagement.

Additionally, we need to maintain a strong Singapore society. Changes in population composition, technology and connectivity will only further increase global and cross-cultural interactions. It is important for Singaporeans to have the knowledge, skills, outlook and mind-set to engage effectively for these interactions to be positive.

But a global outlook does not imply sacrificing local perspectives. A strong Singapore society requires Singaporeans to think "glocally" — to be at the same time a global as well as a Singapore citizen, with a sense of commitment and belonging to the country.

Q7: How can Singaporeans reach out to the global community and make a positive impact?

Singaporeans can seek out information and opportunities from relevant volunteer and non-profit organisations such as the Singapore International Foundation.

At schools or in work organisations in Singapore, there are many structured, international initiatives such as internships, community service activities and corporate social responsibility programmes. They provide excellent experiential opportunities for learning from and engaging with the global community to make a positive impact.

Singaporeans who have colleagues and friends of various nationalities can also make good use of their accessibility of global communities and networks to gain insights into other cultures. This is more easily achieved through daily interactions with each other.

Q8: What are the key misconceptions that international communities have of Singapore?

Some segments of international communities may still have the misconception that Singaporeans are all conscientious and rule-based conformists who are not courageous enough to think or speak critically. The truth is, Singaporeans are quite heterogeneous, and there are actually many who are able and willing to voice critical comments courageously on issues that matter to them.

But many Singaporeans also do it constructively, and this includes prioritising which issues to focus on, and contextualising the discussion with our values that sometimes may be weighted quite differently from those of other communities.

Q9: From your collaborations with the international community, how do you think their impressions of Singapore have changed?

One great change I've observed from their impressions of Singapore and Singaporeans is that we are not just a bunch of uncreative, obedient conformists. This change in perception often comes about when Singaporeans and foreigners find themselves facing similar problems or challenges in the same work environment. That is why having the opportunity to interact naturally at school, work or in social settings is critical to building quality relationships and developing a climate of trust.

Q10: How have your impressions of the international community changed through collaborating with them?

I now see that within-nationality differences are often larger, and matter more, than the between-nationality differences. I've learnt to view each foreigner as a unique individual, with his or her personal attributes. We need to focus on what the individual actually says and does, and not be too quick to draw conclusions based on the foreigner's nationality group or country of origin.

It is not easy to ignore stereotypes, and they often influence our attitudes and actions implicitly without our awareness. But if we can learn to perceive people as individuals, we will be more effective in our interactions, make better judgments, and produce better outcomes.

Chapter 7

What Does a Highly Liveable Singapore Mean?

Is Singapore a highly liveable place? Some say yes, pointing to its low crime rate, good infrastructure and efficient public services. Others cite findings from global surveys consistently showing that Singapore ranks high in liveability among cities in the world.

For example, in the latest Mercer Quality of Living Survey — in which Vienna ranked top in overall liveability — Singapore was ranked 25th in the list of more than 450 cities surveyed worldwide, and top among the cities in Asia. The overall liveability was based on evaluations on 39 factors grouped into 10 broad categories such as education, housing and health.

But national attitudinal surveys, as well as informal conversations with people from different walks of life, yield a more complex picture. For the majority, the honest answer is likely to be "It depends", when they are asked if Singapore is a highly liveable place.

Liveability varies depending on who the question is put to, but it also depends on what dimensions are referred to. Which aspects of life and living are we talking about? Will making Singapore more liveable for one aspect make it less liveable for another? Is liveability for one segment of the population increasing at the expense of another?

The same group of people, and even the same individual, can have mixed thoughts and emotions about how liveable they find a place to be — Singapore can be highly liveable for some things but not for others.

So, an overall score or a general claim summarising Singapore's liveability will not adequately represent people's actual lived experiences, nor capture the ambivalence they are experiencing. That is why Singapore's position on global surveys on liveability can evoke strong reactions regardless of what, and how much or how little, we know about other cities in the list.

Depending on which specific variables we focus on and what metrics we use, the conclusion on Singapore's liveability and what it means for policymaking can be very different.

All these are related to a more basic point. We tend to think about liveability in terms of objective conditions in the living environment, but fundamentally, it is about people's expectations, evaluations and experiences as they interact with their physical, cultural, social and political environments.

A PEOPLE-CENTRIC APPROACH

Many indicators have been used to measure liveability. There are economic indexes such as gross domestic product per capita and human development indexes such as life expectancy and education levels. Then there are conventional metrics of cost of living and standard of living such as purchasing power, crime rates as well as healthcare, many of which are assessed in global surveys on liveability.

These traditional indicators are relevant to both residents and expatriates when there is a need to make comparisons across cities, especially for human resource functions in expatriate assignments. But they often are not good measures of the actual well-being and quality of life experienced by the people.

A truly people-centric approach to liveability should directly examine and empathise with people's expectations, evaluations and experiences because these influence how people think, feel and act, which in turn influence their life and living in Singapore, and also the relationships between individuals, between groups, and between people and the Government.

Improving people's life and living in Singapore is fundamental for our urban planners and national leaders. This is clear to those well-informed of the history and current focus of urban planning and public policies. But as we look to the future, it is important to have more clarity on what it means to effectively adopt and apply a people-centric approach to liveability.

WHAT REALLY MATTERS

I suggest we focus on three important issues.

Groups are Different

First, ensure that the liveability factors adequately capture the experiences of various segments of the population. We need to be scientific in our analyses and interpretation of findings.

For example, policy deliberations and public discourse on attitudinal survey findings have focused almost exclusively on the comparison of mean scores between groups classified by race, income or some other demographic. We compare group means, and we worry about how this group feels in comparison with that group, concluding that one group finds Singapore less liveable.

But some important differences between groups are unrelated to the group mean scores. Two groups can have the same group mean score but how individual scores vary within each group can be very different. It is the pattern of variation within a group that provides information on the dynamics among the individuals in the group.

Consider this hypothetical case of scores on a five-point rating scale measuring an attitude. Individuals within Group A are in high agreement (almost all gave a rating of 3), individuals within Group B are in high disagreement (about equal numbers gave each of the five possible ratings), and individuals within Group C are in polarised split (about one half of the group gave a rating of 1 and the other half gave a rating of 5). These three groups are clearly different in important ways on this attitude, even though they all yield the same group mean score of 3.

If we fail to consider how this, we will miss important group differences. It will result in misleading inferences from the data. Group means are relevant and can be useful, but we need to stop the fixation on only comparing group means.

Attitudes Can Change

Second, anticipate how needs and wants may change over time and across demographic groups.

This is especially relevant when using surveys to gather public sentiment for town planning. Do not simply take the needs and wants reported in these surveys as given. Instead, consider how they may change, the different demographics, and how environmental change can actually influence people's expectations.

The fact that one's attitudes can change over time obviously means we must not take people's positive liveability ratings for granted, since they may decline in the future. But more important, changes over time matter because they are directly associated with one's evaluations and experiences, which in turn influence their attitudes and actions.

What people are asking themselves is: "In the past few years, what was my experience and quality of life, and what is it now?" It is about comparing our current situation with our own recent past, not the distant past as determined by someone else. When there is a negative discrepancy between now and our recent past, we feel disappointed or angry. This will be the case even if our current state is reasonably well in absolute terms.

So, international rankings on liveability and comparisons of cities can be useful for benchmarking and learning purposes. But we must not over-rely on them to drive public policies and urban planning. Inter-city comparisons are not irrelevant, but often it is the intra-city and intra-individual changes over time that matter more, or most.

Singapore is Both City and Country

Third, understand what it really means for Singapore to be both a global city and a cohesive country. The question is how to ensure that these two goals complement, rather than contradict, each other.

Take the need for foreigners versus need to maintain a strong Singaporean core, and the manifestations in local-foreigner relations. How can we develop environments and ways of life that will enable more emotional attachment and rootedness to the country, for both citizens and non-citizens?

For several years now, I have been advocating what I call "home-in-community" as a building block of a liveable Singapore society. This concept will facilitate liveability discussions on issues such as commitment, social cohesion and local-foreigner relations.

The unifying concept of home-in-community applies to all people in Singapore. For example, we should enhance integration and community development through social interaction, mutual help and volunteerism.

In this way, Singaporeans can feel a strong sense of belonging, national identity and rootedness. Singapore permanent residents can see the community as their current second home, with the potential and prospect of making Singapore their first home by becoming citizens. Non-resident foreigners can see the community as a good transient home-away-from-home — attractive to work and play in, but also worthy enough for them to contribute to.

This sense of home-in-community takes time to develop, but is certainly achievable. What we need is to understand how volunteerism, social interactions, local-foreigner relations and commitment can be integrated in natural settings.

For example, foreigners may volunteer for a cause they are passionate about, but they may also give back to the Singapore community out of a sense of moral obligation and gratitude for what they have benefited from. One way to facilitate this is to create opportunities for locals and foreigners to interact in the same community, where foreigners can contribute because they feel they ought to or want to, not because they need to.

By building social relationships between locals and foreigners through meaningful personal interactions within a mixed community, foreigners are likely to develop personal attachments and positive experiences that lead to emotional commitment to Singapore.

It also helps local-foreigner relations and social cohesion. The positive interactions and personal contributions by all will help both Singaporeans and foreigners appreciate what they have in common, understand how their different backgrounds can complement each other, and see one another as individuals rather than as a member of the outgroup.

The emphasis on home-in-community will help us examine liveability from both personal and collective perspectives. Public discussions and policy deliberations on liveability will be more meaningful and constructive because they are more contextualised and inclusive.

Home-in-community involves people's social interactions, social reciprocity and trust, emotional attachment, sense of belonging and rootedness to the place.

These are important socio-psychological resources that we can build to enable the individual and the community to solve problems and achieve desired goals. They are also the bases that enhance and sustain liveability.

Liveability in Singapore is more complex than we think. Beware of sweeping generalisations on how liveable this place is, or is not.

But however complicated the concept of liveability and its measurement, we can better understand and enhance liveability in Singapore if we adhere to two basic guiding principles.

The first is that liveability is about people's expectations, evaluations and experiences, and it is their actual lived experiences that matter. The second is that Singapore is a highly liveable place when we are proud to call it home.

Chapter 8

Too Much of a Good Thing — When Virtue Becomes a Vice

It may be over-exercising, eating a favourite dish too often or being on a long boat cruise — we know and feel it when we have "too much of a good thing". This is that experience of something good becoming bad when the amount is excessive or when we do too much of it.

Too much of a desirable thing that is otherwise enjoyable or beneficial can end up in unpleasant experiences, even harmful consequences. Not just in exercise, food and travel, but also in daily situations. Keep making your password more complex to increase security and you end up having difficulty accessing your computer. Or think about what happens when you spend too much time with your partner.

In these situations, the unpleasant experience is personal and immediate, although others interacting with us may know about it only later, or if we tell them about it.

But there is another set of actions that we engage in, with excessive good becoming bad, which others see immediately. And they see it much more clearly than we do, if we eventually realise it at all. These are actions we exhibit from having too much of a positive attribute, or a positive attitude. Put simply, when our virtue becomes vice.

POSITIVE ATTRIBUTES BECOMING NEGATIVE

We categorise personal attributes into good versus bad. We value self-confidence and discourage self-doubt. We say be conscientious, not careless. And we take pride in courage and despise cowardice. But when confidence, conscientiousness or courage overflows, we become maladaptive.

When people are overconfident, they often do too much. Someone overconfident of his public speaking skills will overestimate the audience's interest in what he has to say, and their positive impression of his delivery. The speech then goes on longer than necessary, offering more arguments than needed, with more illustrations than planned. The overconfidence is self-defeating — the goal to persuade or awe the audience is not achieved. It may even backfire.

Conscientiousness is another positive attribute we can have too much of. A conscientious person not only puts in effort, he also attends to details and perseveres despite slow or even no progress. But when someone is excessively conscientious, what should be a meticulous action becomes obsessive-compulsive behaviour. And when there are good reasons to stop, his dogged determination to persevere on the same course is stubborn behaviour, a failure to adapt.

The courage to speak the unpleasant truth or speak up against unfairness is a positive attribute. Courage is all the more precious when the cost of speaking up is high. But too much courage hurts more than helps. It can cause someone to have little or no inhibition in expressing and explicating whatever is in one's mind. It becomes impulsivity, maladaptive forthrightness and poor situational judgment ability.

Now and then, we may be too conscientious or too courageous. But it is overconfidence that everyone should pay more attention to, because it is the most prevalent.

OVERCONFIDENCE AND OPTIMISM BIAS

Overconfidence is ubiquitous when people make judgments and decisions. In numerous studies on confidence, conducted in different cultures using diverse tasks, participants were asked to rate how good they think they are, either in absolute terms or relative to others. Invariably, be it driving skills or teaching performance, the results show that the large majority of participants — often close to 80 per cent — believe they are better than the median. This is statistically impossible because objectively only 50 per cent of the sample are above the median score.

Research also shows that people are overconfident about the accuracy of their forecasts, whether it is predicting the stock market performance or their firm's profits.

There is a substantial gap between what people think they know and what they actually know. Research shows that this disconnect between self-belief and reality is larger for people with higher academic achievements, experts in various fields, and those in positions of authority and power.

Confirmatory bias is the human tendency to selectively seek out information to confirm one's preconceived belief or position. If it is the mother of all biases, then overconfidence is the father. Together, these two biases have given birth to a host of other cognitive biases that pervade human judgment and decision-making.

For example, overconfidence produces optimism bias. This is the tendency to expect positive futures regardless of evidence and logic. Optimism bias is maladaptive. It is an unrealistic belief and hope that a future outcome will be positive, when such a future is implausible.

Optimism bias in planning can have serious negative consequences. Bad predictions and, therefore, decisions can lead to large investment losses, underused public infrastructure or not-so-smart cities that are not resilient to cybersecurity crises.

WHEN A POSITIVE ATTITUDE IS EXCESSIVE

We can also be excessive in our positive attitudes towards others. Take trust, for instance. High trust can be mistrust — trusting when we should not. The consequences can be disastrous when we have extremely high trust in people who are not trustworthy, especially when you trust not just in someone's competence, but also their integrity and benevolence when these are absent.

When trust level is excessively high, we do not question claims and assumptions, nor ask for facts and supporting evidence. And transparency and accountability are not on our mind. All these make us highly vulnerable to exploitation when we mistrust manipulative characters.

Contrary to popular discourse on trust, distrust — which simply means low trust — is not always a bad thing. But the best antidote to being overly trusting is not to embrace destructive cynicism. Instead, develop a healthy scepticism. This is a mindset of critical thinking like that of a good scientist — rationally questioning assumptions and objectively evaluating claims, giving priority to facts and evidence.

Another positive attitude that can become excessive occurs when people work together in a team. We use the term "team player" to compliment a member who agrees with the rest of the team or compromises his position to achieve group consensus. And we call the one who does not go along with the team a disagreeable or dogmatic individual.

Normally, an agreeable attitude helps team functioning. It maintains harmonious relations among members and builds group cohesion, and these contribute to team morale and performance. But we know from the research on teams, and also many real-life examples in business and politics, that too much value placed on agreement and group consensus will lead to groupthink. This is the phenomenon where a highly cohesive team makes bad decisions because team members withheld dissenting views to go along with majority opinion.

In groupthink, members agree and do not express a different view due to pressures to conform or maintain social harmony. Groupthink happens most often in teams that value consensus and cohesion. And also when the team climate either forces or nudges members to keep quiet, agree with the leader and senior team members or express only views that they think those in power want to hear.

SELF-REFLECT, TAKE CONSTRUCTIVE STEPS

If virtue can become vice, how can one take steps to still value virtue and do good?

Clearly, we should not pretend that we do not have those positive attributes and attitudes — that will be false modesty. What we need is to know our limits, so that we can do better with our virtues.

Knowing our limits means knowing when to stop or pause, well before our positive attribute or attitude crosses the limit and becomes negative. This, however, does not call for moderation or a limiting restraint, like in exercising and eating. Instead, what is required is a self-reflection process.

By self-reflecting, we figure out what to do, and when and how to pursue a course of action. It involves asking ourselves what is the issue at hand and its practical context, when to apply which positive attribute or attitude, who are the people involved, and how we can do things better.

For example, the answer to preventing overconfidence and optimism bias is not to moderate by reducing confidence and optimism. We cannot be effective problem solvers if we encourage self-doubt and pessimism, which are themselves maladaptive. Instead, self-reflect and take steps to behave constructively.

How might this process look like? Back to my example on overconfidence in public speaking skills. Unfamiliar with the topic of your speech? Then plan your content and delivery. Humble yourself to seek input from knowledgeable others. Remember that you actually know less than you thought.

If the topic is familiar, decide which key points to share and stick to them during delivery. Beware of the tendency to exhibit your knowledge by bringing up more information and illustrations than planned. Otherwise, you will find it difficult to keep to time, disrupting the programme and annoying everyone. Not only that, your well-intended detailed accounts may come across as incessant and tiresome at best, and condescending at worst.

Which is why it is important to know your audience. No one likes an arrogant speaker, but a well-informed and knowledgeable audience gets most riled up when it perceives patronising superiority. Even more so if its members were not there by volition to listen to you.

Ignorance plus arrogance may make one a target of gossip and the butt of jokes. The power of negativity bias can amplify the criticisms as they multiply. This leads to a negative spiral of reactions and evaluations, never mind that such a response is objectively unfair to the one targeted.

So, put simply, understand people's emotions and what they may experience, and learn to see things from another's perspective.

Finally, after each speech, seek feedback from people likely to tell you the truth, especially those who do not share your background or viewpoints. Spend less time with those who agree with you on everything.

We can extrapolate this example on public speaking to other areas and virtues.

In sum, my point in this essay is a simple one. It does not matter who you are — all of us need to guard against the perils of excessiveness. When we self-reflect and consciously take constructive steps, we can prevent the negatives that result from having too much of a good thing.

When we can stop virtue from becoming vice, then we can develop positive attributes and attitudes to make a positive difference for ourselves and to the lives of others.

Chapter 9

How to Take Feedback Seriously

It is a common practice these days for people to assess or react to a product they buy, a service they receive, or performance or activity they took part in. Giving feedback has become very much a way of life.

Feedback is not restricted to customer service or performance appraisal situations. It can also refer to public reactions to an incident, expressed as evaluations, emotions and concerns.

People may have views on an incident, and also how they perceive the incident was handled or is being handled. Some recent cases come to mind — such as national servicemen training deaths, the SingHealth cyberattack and the HIV Registry data leak.

Public expressions on these matters are valuable feedback that reflects and reveals much. They are unsolicited real-life reactions to actual specific incidents and how they are handled. We hear the reactions in informal conversations. We read the public comments written in mainstream media and posted on social media, with a mix of reflective and visceral reactions.

A noteworthy commentary is a recent editorial in the local Chinese daily Lianhe Zaobao that raised serious questions of leadership complacency, accountability and public trust in Government. The commentary, together with others, elicited a response from Finance Minister Heng Swee Keat last Saturday, published in both Lianhe Zaobao and The Straits Times.

Mr Heng stated that the Singapore Government has not "gone slack", such as becoming complacent and failing to hold senior people accountable when things went wrong. He reiterated that its leaders "will not flinch from taking a hard look at ourselves each time there is a failure, and doing whatever is necessary to put things right."

SOLDER DEATHS, DATA LEAK

Earlier this week in Parliament, Defence Minister Ng Eng Hen and Health Minister Gan Kim Yong responded to questions on the recent soldier training deaths and the HIV data leak, respectively. The ministers provided some additional details to what were already made known to the public since the news broke.

The critical information on how the training deaths of the two national servicemen (Liu Kai in last November and Aloysius Pang in January) occurred, and why, are currently not known. Hopefully, the two committees of inquiry will provide thorough and clear answers, and soon.

For the HIV data leak, we can expect differences in views among the public on the Health Ministry's "judgment call" in decisions and actions on when and what to tell who, with regard to the data leak. The ministry's statements also spark debate on the security of personal data the public entrusted to the Government. It also raises the issue of HIV and the stigma around it, which influenced decisions on whether to inform the individuals affected and the general public of a data leak.

Some will continue to have questions on how the event unfolded, the coordination among government agencies involved and their interactions and investigations with the two individuals in the centre of the data leak — American Mikhy Farrera Brochez and Singaporean Ler Teck Siang.

The HIV data leak incident is still evolving, with fresh information to emerge, and possible further public exposure of the leaked data. Also, not all of the affected individuals have been informed that their personal data was leaked.

Public reactions to the soldier deaths and data leak incident will continue. And they may become more negative or positive. The Government and its related agencies will have to decide how to respond to the evolving reactions to these recent adverse incidents, and future ones. Will the impending government-public interactions make things better or worse? It is useful to take a hard look at the feedback process applicable to previous and future exchanges.

MALADAPTIVE RESPONSES TO NEGATIVE FEEDBACK

If we misconstrue valid negative feedback and dismiss them as ignorant or malicious, we will fail to identify our mistakes to take remedial action. We will be positively reinforced to reiterate and repeat our maladaptive actions.

It will also create unnecessary ambivalence or distrust in the relationship with the feedback givers. We will also miss out potentially good ideas and solutions that can arise from addressing the issues associated with the negative feedback. The consequence is a rapid spiral of negative outcomes.

The first human reaction to negative feedback is unpleasant emotions such as anger and disappointment. This is followed quickly by defensive responses to justify our actions or inactions.

For example, when making sense of our failures, we often attribute too little weight to ourselves and too much weight to external factors such as the situation and the behaviours of others. Our defensive responses often include recounting the many good things we have done. We end up citing many things that, while good, are irrelevant to the negative feedback given.

Sometimes we are not defensive, but our initially sensible response becomes maladaptive when over-done or not well communicated.

It is true that everyone has a part to play in enhancing a positive climate for safety in military training and a societal culture of non-discrimination in treatment of people with HIV. But if we overemphasise collective responsibility or highlight it when the critical issue is something else, we will be perceived as attempting to detract or shift blame. We end up giving the public impression that we are actually saying, "It's your fault too" or "It's your fault".

Another sensible response that can go wrong is emphasising that no system is perfect. The reminder is appropriate if the negative feedback stems from an unrealistic expectation that there must be zero errors. But the emphasis backfires when the negative feedback comes about because of a series of similar or seemingly related errors.

The overemphasis occurs when we fail to appreciate how public expectations evolve and how this relates to negative public reactions. It is a myth to believe that people expect everything to be perfect and have zero tolerance for any mistakes.

People form expectations partly based on what they have experienced routinely. When unmet expectations upset people, it is often because their routine standards are frustrated — not because the standards did not achieve a perfect score. They react when lapses have personal consequences or severe outcomes that they can see affecting themselves, others or society.

Attempting to moderate public expectations or address unmet expectations by emphasising that perfection is impossible, or that human lapses do occur, misses the point. In fact, trying to do so will only lead to perceptions that the Government is lacking in empathy, disconnected from ground sentiments or trying to shift the blame to alleged public irrationality.

What seems like a sensible response becomes maladaptive when we say the right thing at the wrong time or in the wrong way.

TAKING FEEDBACK SERIOUSLY

How then to respond adaptively when people give us negative feedback? I suggest 11 basic principles.

- Spend less time listening to people who give you only positive feedback or agree with you on everything. This creates delusion of positivity and maladaptive responses to valuable negative feedback.

- Be honestly humble and seek more feedback from those who do not have similar background or views as you. Be open to the possibility that your view, conclusion or position may be mistaken.
- Understand that it is human to experience unpleasant emotions when the feedback is negative, but don't let the emotions affect your responses.
- Don't be defensive. It is not necessary to recount all the good things — it backfires when they are irrelevant to the core concerns in the feedback.
- Don't be patronising. People are not irrational and unrealistic in their expectations. Understand how recent incidents and related observations may have led to unmet expectations.
- Don't jump to conclusions. Ask people to elaborate on their negative feedback, which may reveal additional important feedback or misunderstanding of facts from the individual giving or receiving the feedback.
- Understand the emotions and experiences of the people involved including those providing the feedback. Learn to see things from their perspectives.
- Be transparent and accountable. Provide an honest and full account of what actually happened and how it happened. Explain and justify the actual considerations that went into the decisions made. Hold the right individuals responsible for their deeds and decisions. This must be done without fear or favour, both actual and perceived.
- Reinforce the value of integrity and position on zero tolerance for wrongdoings. Demonstrate with action, and not just give words of assurance that there is will to correct mistakes and get things right.

- Be prompt in responding. Lengthy delays and releasing information in a piecemeal fashion and at different times with no clear reasons will fuel cynicism. Preliminary statements or accounts may be useful, but they should not come across as attempts to influence fact-finding and bias conclusions.
- Revise and adapt your responses in the light of reasonable feedback and new information that are credible and critical.

BECOMING BETTER

We may say the above principles are obvious, and some leaders are already explicitly espousing one or more of these principles in public engagement. Yet, most of us don't practise them enough, well enough, or at all. We may even be repeatedly acting in maladaptive ways that go against these principles.

Advocating but not practising effective responses, plus repeated inadequacies, add to the angst and disappointment experienced by those who give feedback when they see that the feedback does not work. This is most unfortunate, especially when people at both ends of the feedback share the common goal of achieving better performance and outcomes in future.

So, we need to learn to self-reflect. Be honest and humble. Be clear, courageous and constructive when responding to feedback. Take concrete corrective actions responsibly, and with accountability. We can prevent many inadequacies in feedback response and their unintended negative consequences. Adopt a principled approach to feedback response so that things become better — preventable adverse incidents will occur less frequently and we can co-create solutions to problems.

As people continue to give feedback, they may learn how to deliver it more effectively. Meanwhile, we need to take the feedback given seriously.

Chapter 10

The "Seven S" Approach to Subject-Based Banding in Schools

By 2024, the system of streaming secondary school students into Express, Normal (Academic) or Normal (Technical) based on their PSLE results will be replaced by subject-based banding, or SBB, where students take a combination of subjects from three different bands based on their strengths.

SBB is already practised in primary schools. In secondary schools, SBB is now used for the four core subjects — the two languages, mathematics and science. In 2024, SBB will be expanded to cover all subjects in secondary schools. Implementing SBB at secondary schools is a logical step based on pedagogical customisation.

Fundamentally, what is at stake is the future of our children. Many people have welcomed the end of streaming as it has been practised for 40 years, but many also worry that the new SBB system will similarly become stigmatising, as students will still be placed on three tracks of G1, G2 and G3 in secondary school.

However, we should avoid jumping to conclusions because of anxiety, angst or assumptions. In policymaking and implementation, and also public engagement and discussion, we should approach issues objectively and with an open mind. So, we need to understand SBB and its related issues in the context of the science and practice of human motivation and performance, which is the focus of this essay.

First, both streaming and SBB share the same underlying principle that students be given the appropriate level of academic demands that suit their abilities and aptitudes, so that they can learn at a pace that works well for them and enables them to realise their potential. This principle is supported by research showing that when we can set goals that are concrete and specific, and also difficult but realistically achievable, we will be motivated to perform well to pursue those goals.

Streaming did not take into account certain elements that can be found or easier practised in SBB.

I will call these the "Seven S" elements of education — specific abilities, suitability, self-concepts, stigma, student-centric schools, societal attitudes and subjective well-being. Done right, the new SBB system has the potential to enhance our education system significantly.

SPECIFIC ABILITIES

Human beings have varied skills in different areas. Relying only on general academic ability misses out on important information on an individual's profile of strengths and weaknesses on different abilities.

The old streaming system categorises students broadly into two general academic ability levels — high versus low — by taking the composite score of performance across different subjects. A student who has great potential in one subject but not in others could be placed on the lower-ability Normal stream, while another student who does reasonably well in all subjects but excels in none could go to the higher-ability Express stream.

The problem is exacerbated if the Normal stream environment is not conducive to developing the student's specific ability in the subject he does well in and, worse, if it is overall demotivating for the student to perform academically.

SBB, on the other hand, treats each subject independently. Students can take a combination of subjects at different levels depending on their aptitude. SBB thus provides useful information on the student's profile of abilities and achievements, and the necessary information for the student's academic development.

SUITABILITY

An important element in SBB is suitability, which is the student-subject match. Not only does this recognise a student's specific ability in an area, it also helps him develop interest and passion in it.

We are more motivated to learn and do well in a subject area that we have interest in, and passion and deep skills are then likely to be developed. Research has shown that, across all fields and work domains, true experts are knowledgeable and skillful due to dedicated hard work but they enjoy putting in the effort because of their interest and passion in the activities.

Such interest-based and passion-driven motivation is intrinsic and does not require extrinsic motivators like punishments or rewards.

SELF-CONCEPTS

How students view themselves and their time in school is important to determine how they develop in life.

SBB can improve the way students view themselves, as it encourages them to take subjects at a level they are suited for. Most people cannot be good in almost all areas. The subject-based focus in SBB helps students develop self-efficacy in selected areas. Self-efficacy refers to the belief that one can mobilise resources and work to accomplish task demands and solve problems in a specific domain.

Research has consistently shown that self-efficacy predicts performance and success at work. As self-efficacy develops, a positive cycle results: students feel capable and become motivated to get more involved in activities related to the subject. They may learn to figure out what they are best at, enhancing self-insight.

Over time, self-efficacy and self-insight contribute to self-esteem, which is the student's overall evaluation and feeling of his own worth. This will be a stark contrast to the feeling of inadequacy that students feel as they strive to perform well in all areas and end up not doing as well as they could have in specific areas.

STIGMA

The stigma associated with social labelling resulting from streaming has been corrosive in many people's lives and for society.

The new SBB system can go a long way to reduce stigma in secondary education. In SBB, it is still possible to compare and rank students according to the combinations of the three possible bands (G1, G2 or G3) for each subject. But as most students will be taking a mix of subjects at different levels, any comparison requires detailed analysis of the students' subject profiles.

Moreover, in the SBB system, most students will be crossing banding levels when they move from one subject to another within a week of classroom lessons. This means they will not be confined to an ability category and labelled accordingly, unlike the case in Normal or Express streaming where students are placed into clear groupings, creating the perception of "us versus them".

Even if students and parents try to compare, rank and categorise students by their overall ability, it will be difficult and unnatural to do so in the SBB system. Of course, SBB is no guarantee against unhealthy groupings and social exclusion. We need naturalistic environments for students of different backgrounds to mix and interact, so that they learn and play together as peers.

Such interaction helps counter stereotypes and reduce stigma. Not only that, it can develop altruism, compassion, ability to empathise and see things from another's perspective, skills to collaborate and work effectively with others, social harmony and social capital.

STUDENT-CENTRIC SCHOOLS

As schools develop the curriculum, logistics and culture for SBB, they must be student-centric, giving top priority to the student's learning process and personal development.

Ground feedback must be heeded: principals, teachers and school staff may be committed, but they require support and coaching for things to work as intended.

Educators and policymakers must live up to the belief in diverse abilities, interests and passion associated with different subject areas. We fail if we send the signal that some subject areas are inherently better than others regardless of the student's profile.

Being student-centric also means recognising that students develop at a different pace, even within a subject. Students should be able to move across bands in the same subject at appropriate times. The bands within a subject should be reasonably porous.

SOCIETAL ATTITUDES

Across sectors and industries, rapid changes are occurring in the nature of work. General academic ability won't be enough, as employers seek workers with wider skillsets and adaptive traits to function in multi-disciplinary teams.

Students and parents need to take these changes seriously and adapt quickly to them.

One shift needed is from a fixed mindset to a growth mindset in thinking about ability. A fixed mindset assumes ability is fixed and that one must come to terms with a child's weakness.

A growth mindset helps the child explore and develop his interests and abilities. This takes time and requires an adaptive learning environment that is child-centric. To develop a growth mindset, learn to praise and focus on children's effort. Do not just highlight how smart or talented they are.

Parents and schools also need to become more child-centric. This means discerning what is good or bad for the child, and not constantly comparing how the child performs relative to other children. Many issues concerning comparison, competition and being child-centric apply to teacher and educator attitudes as well.

SUBJECTIVE WELL-BEING

SBB has the potential to help students develop positive subjective well-being. Such feelings come from satisfaction over met needs, expectations and preferences, experiencing positive rather than negative emotions, and having a sense of personal meaning derived from having the autonomy and ability to pursue and live a fulfilling life.

An education system with the traits highlighted above — such as being student-centric, suited to students' abilities and not stigmatising — helps students feel better about themselves.

When their learning encounters are positive, students experience high subjective well-being, which results in higher motivation, better performance and more pro-social behaviours. Encounters and experiences in the formative years at secondary school, together with their competency and character development, contribute to students' "can do" ability and "will do" attitude that help them lead successful and fulfilling lives when they enter the workforce and function independently and interdependently in society.

WHAT IT ALL MEANS

If we attend to the seven elements of education, implementing SBB will benefit all students in terms of learning, assessment and development, regardless of academic ability and performance levels. We can then be hopeful that positive changes will occur, and sooner than later. But if we think no systematic effort is needed, trivialise important issues and simply assume that everything will naturally fall in place, then SBB will lead to many unintended negative consequences.

Whoever we are, it is self-defeating if we disregard facts and insist that SBB is just old wine in new bottles.

And it will be a self-fulfilling prophecy if we externalise all problems to the purported power or weakness of others, the situation or the system, and construe students as either helpless victims or hopeless individuals with no possibility of improving.

Of course, many problems are not of our own doing. But as we hope that others, systems and society change for the better, we should revisit our assumptions, arguments, attitudes and actions.

Whether you are a student, parent, educator, employer, worker or policymaker, as an individual, we can initiate action and change, innovate methods and practices, and inculcate positive values and attitudes in ourselves and those around us.

Chapter 11

Why Smart Leaders Fail

In Singapore, when leaders in the public service or government-linked organisations are found wanting, people in their private conversations sometimes go: "Those scholars ..."

In Singapore, "scholars" often refer to academically excellent students who take up government-funded scholarships to study at top universities and return to high-flying careers in the public sector. When people make remarks about "scholars", one negative connotation is that having high academic ability (indicated by top academic grades) has caused one to think and act in ways that reflect poor leadership and ineffective performance.

But does top academic ability actually imply poor leadership? And in Singapore's context, does the current system of selecting and developing leaders rely too much on academic (and cognitive) abilities and is inadequate in capturing critical non-academic factors? More generally, does having high academic ability help or hurt work performance, or when does it help or hurt?

Answers to these questions have implications for practical decisions such as selecting leaders or employees, designing systems and programmes to appraise individuals and develop leaders, and when or who to give more or fewer leadership responsibilities to.

MORE OPEN DISCUSSIONS

These questions on leadership and other topics were discussed at the recent Behavioural Sciences Institute Conference, attended by 300 participants from the public, private and people sectors. Held two months ago with the theme "Much more than academic abilities", the conference proceedings have been documented in a book published by World Scientific.

A week after the conference, Mr Chan Chun Sing, the Minister-in-charge of the Public Service, said in Parliament on Feb 28 that educational qualifications, while useful as a "valid proxy", will not be sufficient for selecting future leaders in the Singapore Public Service. He added that the Government is looking for individuals with initiative, creativity and the ability to be a team player.

And just last week, in his speech at the administrative service promotion ceremony, Minister Chan elaborated on some non-academic attributes, including integrity and accountability. He urged the public service to review the way it selects and develops its leaders. He also noted that the head of the civil service and the Public Service Commission have already initiated various streams of work to do so.

We can expect more open discussions on leadership in Singapore, not just in the public service but also in other sectors. To shed more light rather than generate mere heat on the issues, we should draw on experiences in practice and evidence from scientific research.

EXPERIENCE AND EVIDENCE

First, consider our personal experiences. Many who have interacted with different leaders can name leaders they look up to, as well as those they would stay away from. While leaders may be similarly and highly intelligent — academically speaking — our experiences tell us that they can differ quite widely on the spectrum of leader effectiveness as we compare and contrast them.

At the same time, those familiar with how the public sector selects and develops its leaders would know that there are real efforts to look beyond academic abilities or achievements. Values, motivations, personality traits and other non-academic attributes are taken seriously. They are measured and considered, although in varying degrees across organisations.

Put simply, many could say from their personal experiences that leaders share similar traits but are also highly diverse.

Second, we know a lot about leader effectiveness from established evidence produced by scientific research and consulting practice, both globally and locally.

Academic abilities are not just important in school settings — research has established that they are also critical for leadership and performance in problem-solving contexts involving intellectual demands. Examples of such demands are logical thinking, abstract thinking and academic-related knowledge such as knowing how to interpret numerical data.

But research has also shown that, very often, academic abilities cannot be the only or even most important contributory factor for successful performance. In addition, academic ability does not determine if a person also has strong non-academic attributes that lead to good performance; it is independent of such attributes.

Indeed, there is clear evidence that many critical processes and outcomes at work are not dependent, or are less dependent, on academic abilities. Examples include work engagement, team functioning, innovation, crisis management, adaptive performance and resilience.

Finally, leader effectiveness is highly dependent on various non-academic abilities and attributes, which can interact in important ways to affect leader attitudes and actions and, in turn, influence people's reactions and support. This is a critical point, so let me illustrate with research that I conducted several years ago in Singapore.

JUDGING PRACTICAL SITUATIONS

In one study of public-sector officers (published in the Journal of Applied Psychology), I used validated instruments to measure each officer's proactive personality and situational judgement effectiveness. Proactive personality is the disposition to speak up, seek opportunities, initiate things and get things done, persevere until one sees changes occur, and act to change the status quo situation. Situational judgement effectiveness, or SJE, refers to an individual's ability to make effective judgements in practical situations. It involves attending to the important cues in a given practical situation, making sense of what the situation means and how it may evolve, and making decisions and responding to the situation effectively.

I also measured the officers' work outcomes such as job performance, job satisfaction, organisational commitment and organisational citizenship behaviour. The study showed that the same results were replicated across all these and other important work outcomes.

I not only looked at whether an officer was high on proactive personality and SJE, but also assessed how effective or ineffective such traits are in their work outcomes. When an officer with a proactive personality achieves good work outcomes, it is considered adaptive to be high on that proactive trait. When being proactive results in poor outcomes, then being high on the trait is considered maladaptive.

Here is the key finding: Whether being high on proactive personality is adaptive or maladaptive (meaning whether it helps or hurts the work outcomes) is dependent on how high or low one's level of SJE is.

Among officers who were high on SJE, the more proactive ones did better than the less proactive ones. But among those who were low on SJE, the more proactive ones did worse than the less proactive ones. In other words, being proactive actually hurts officers who are not effective at judging situations.

This might seem to be counterintuitive until common sense kicks in: A highly proactive officer who wants to effect change at work, for example, will not succeed if he has poor SJE because he is not able to understand what matters more or most in the practical situation and relevant work environment. He may, for example, not realise that the organisational structure, process or people involved are not suited or ready for that change he wants to introduce.

The practical implications are clearly serious. It means we cannot just select or reward individuals who are highly proactive. Being more proactive is positive only if the individuals are also effective in judging situations. If they are ineffective in judging situations (low on SJE), then it is worse if they are more proactive.

SITUATIONAL JUDGEMENT MATTERS

Like proactive personality, top academic ability can help or hurt, depending on one's level of SJE.

High levels of academic ability and proactivity certainly help for those who also have high SJE. But an academically smart person who is proactive but has poor SJE can be a liability when put in top leadership positions.

It is not difficult to have leaders who are both academically smart and proactive — most leaders in Singapore already are. But we need to pay much more attention to SJE when selecting and developing leaders. This point is relevant to the effectiveness of political leaders, regardless of the country they are governing.

Take the example of citizens feeling that they do not have a say in decisions that affect them because they perceive that an important decision or policy lacks transparency. If political leaders fail to address this critical aspect in the situation or even identify it, then there will be trust erosion and some of their proactive behaviour may backfire.

That is why, before proactively galvanising citizens to work towards a goal or explaining why they need to change their mindsets, political leaders should put on their SJE hat and address citizens' concerns about the policymaking process.

My key point in this essay is this: When it comes to leadership across all sectors, it really does not matter what the person's position in the organisation is or who the person is — the ability to judge practical situations effectively is critical. An effective leader attends to appropriate cues in a situation and focuses on matters that really matter.

So, when assessing why leaders fail, it is not helpful to have a knee-jerk reaction against "those scholars". Instead, figure out the factors that make this leader fail in this organisation, and then learn how to improve the leadership selection and development system so that we have leaders with much more than academic abilities and proactive traits.

We need leaders who can effectively sense and judge practical situations — the mood of a the people, the culture of an organisation, strengths and weaknesses, and what needs to change — and catalyse change effectively. This will help us to effect positive changes with meaningful impact for ourselves, those around us and our society.

Chapter 12

Why People Self-Sabotage, and How to Stop it

Self-sabotage occurs when we want to achieve a goal and then go about getting in our own way, as if to make sure what we want does not happen. Rationally, it is hard to understand why anyone would do that. In reality, all of us self-sabotage now and then, in varying degrees.

Psychologists study self-sabotage because normal people do it even though it is maladaptive, which seems puzzling.

Self-sabotage can occur in two types of situations. The first concerns self-discipline. The second is in interactions with others. Most of us are familiar with the first but much less so with the second. But we do need to pay more attention to the latter, which is when we harm ourselves by undermining or destroying our relationships with others.

SELF-DISCIPLINE

But first, let's talk briefly about self-discipline.

Research on "self-handicapping" has shown that people sometimes do things to hurt their own chances of success in order to avoid taking responsibility for their subsequent failures. So, students or workers sometimes choose to play or stay up late, instead of studying or resting, just before an important examination or presentation. When they do poorly, they blame their friends, that glass of beer, Netflix or some external factors rather than their own lack of ability, effort or dedication.

We can think of similar situations like setting a goal to exercise and lose weight and then going about with activities and eating habits that are self-defeating in achieving the goal.

In these self-discipline situations, a key psychological process underlying self-sabotage behaviours is the need to protect one's self-esteem in anticipation of potential failure. Studies have shown that although self-esteem may remain intact temporarily this way, such behaviours in the long run exact long-term costs.

Not only is there failure to attain the desired goal, the real cause of failure is masked. The negative emotions, thoughts and outcomes associated with goal failure will also eventually erode self-esteem.

There are strategies, based on evidence, to avoid this trap. Examples include focusing on how we can control our own effort and discipline to affect outcomes, learning to avoid procrastination, engaging in self-monitoring, and setting goals that are specific, challenging and realistic.

SELF-OTHERS INTERACTION

Self-sabotage can happen during interactions with others, be it in relationships in our personal life, at the workplace or in politics. Self-sabotage in these interactions begins when we say and do things that lead others to have negative perceptions of us.

Let's be clear on a distinction. Avoiding actions that create negative perceptions is not the same as being dishonest in interactions or being populist and pandering to prevailing public sentiments. Being tactful is not inconsistent with being truthful.

Note, though, that it hurts instead of help when we say and do the right thing but in the wrong way or at the wrong time. An example of this is when a supervisor correctly points out the mistakes of his subordinate but not in a constructive way. The supervisor may be factually right but self-sabotages by going overboard in scolding the subordinate in the presence of his co-workers. Not only does he fail to achieve his goal — for example, getting everyone to learn from the mistake made — he ends up creating in others negative perceptions of him as a person, rightly or wrongly.

His action may end up giving the impression of incivility and exaggeration, or worse still, bullying and self-righteousness. And he may not even be aware of it. This is partly because not many, if any, would tell those in power when they are wrong, for fear of the repercussions. The problem is compounded when a person in authority surrounds himself with people who would say only positive things to please him. The self-defeating behaviours get reinforced; the goals keep getting thwarted.

Of course, people do not plan to sabotage themselves, which is why when people see that their actions have contributed to unintended negative consequences, they ask themselves, "Why did I do that?" and think counterfactually, "If only …"

Some do gain self-awareness from these questions and learn to do better the next time. But for those inclined to blame others, they are likely to commit similar mistakes repeatedly and develop the habit of self-sabotage.

STEPS TO STOP SELF-SABOTAGE

How to counter self-sabotage? Based on research evidence, I suggest three steps. These seemingly obvious steps are worth reinforcing and reflecting. We often hear them espoused rather than see them in action.

Be Humble

Some counsellors have said that addressing self-sabotage begins with recognising its signs, such as deterioration in our relationships with others. But the real first step is to learn to be humble. Without humility, we will never truly recognise the signs of self-sabotage in our interactions with others, even when everyone else around us see them clearly.

Being humble is less about impression management and more about being aware that we really don't have all the answers and that others, especially collectively, may know many things that we don't. That is why, be genuine when consulting others — not just to identify solutions, but also to understand the nature of the problems.

So, being humble means starting with the premise that you don't know everything, you may not be the best, and you need the help of others. It also means accepting that we may have made mistakes so that we can more easily identify, acknowledge and learn from them.

Be Honest

Honesty in relationships is about telling others the truth. Lying, misrepresenting facts and covering up will backfire when the truth is discovered.

Honesty is also about being objective. Do not deceive by presenting one-sided arguments, armed with selective data chosen only because it is consistent with the position you want to advocate. People can see through the biases soon, if not immediately, since no one has monopoly over all relevant information and expertise.

To be honest and objective means to ascertain facts and evaluate analyses, arguments and perspectives in a dispassionate manner, without fear or favour. This often involves taking a moment to suspend our personal beliefs and subjective preferences.

It also means revisiting our own assumptions, considering the weight of the evidence, and seriously entertaining the possibility that others are right and we are wrong. In the light of new evidence or information that is credible and critical, have the intellectual honesty and political courage to revise our prior position.

Honesty is especially important when we interact with others in a feedback process. When giving feedback, do not sugar-coat, but do not be offensive. Be courageous and constructive. When taking feedback, do not pretend to agree, but do not be defensive. Be truthful but tactful.

How we give and take feedback is as important as the feedback content. A constructive feedback process is critical for the feedback to be effective.

Be Humane

Sometimes, we self-sabotage our relationships because we don't treat people in a humane manner when dealing with disagreements.

Among the many dimensions of humane treatment, being kind and being empathetic are two important ones that directly affect the management of disagreement.

When we have a strong disagreement with others, don't say things just to make them look bad or embarrass them. If we find fault on every detail, we come across as doing a witch-hunt. It is self-defeating because the key points we want to make will get diluted, if not lost, in the details.

We end up looking non-objective and being seen as taking things personally when we should not. It backfires badly if what we say are not exposing actual wrongdoing but only serve to disparage others instead of addressing the substantive issues that matter most.

So, focus on what is important and not the relatively trivial. Choose which battles to fight. It is wise to be gracious and generous in spirit when doing so does not compromise the truth.

When we treat others who disagree strongly with us in a humane manner, the kindness we show is a strength and not a weakness.

Evidence and experience tell us that when we treat others kindly and with respect and dignity, we can make everyone more reasonable and focus more on the positives, cool a contentious issue into a non-issue, and earn public goodwill from observers.

Empathy is another effective counter to self-sabotage in relationships. Empathy involves considering how others feel and appreciating their concerns, constraints, aspirations, resources and experiences.

When we get outside our own perspectives and try to understand the position and frame of reference of those who disagree with us, we are likely to become more informed, wiser, less impulsive and more equipped to deal with disagreements.

TAKING SELF-SABOTAGE SERIOUSLY

Our negative behaviours in self-sabotage are influenced by our negative emotions like anxiety, anger, disappointment and disgust. When we take steps to be humble, honest and humane, we become better in moderating these negative emotions.

We also become more likely to refrain from acting or reacting impulsively in ways that self-sabotage relationships, such as generating more heat to the disagreement through patronising and provocative comments, and saying or doing the right thing in the wrong way or at the wrong time.

The three H steps help us pause and remember the three Rs — refrain, reflect and resolve — so that we can make good progress towards our goal.

It does not matter who we are or how smart we think we are — we are all "capable" of choosing to think, feel and act in ways that defeat our own goals. No one is immune from self-sabotage.

We need to take this seriously, especially in relationships and when interacting with others, because such maladaptive functioning can lead to worse outcomes than we realise. Each thought, emotion and behaviour does not occur in isolation. They result from and lead to one another, spreading into a spiral of negative outcomes.

Be it in our personal life, at work or in politics, the science of self-sabotage can help us stop self-defeating behaviours and learn lessons that enable us to do better in future.

When we are more humble, honest and humane, we are less likely to self-sabotage our relationships with others. This helps us achieve our goals effectively and minimise unintended negative consequences.

Chapter 13

The 5Cs of Beating the Coronavirus Outbreak

For a few weeks now, Singapore's news headlines have been dominated practically daily by case updates and control measures related to the coronavirus disease, now officially known as COVID-19.

To tackle public fear and anxiety, our political leaders promptly release information affecting public health and emphasise that health advisories and decisions on control measures are evidence-based. They reassure the public that there are adequate medical and food supplies.

They also warn against irrational, counterproductive or discriminatory behaviours. They highlight societal values of social harmony, civic-mindedness and altruism.

On Friday last week, Singapore raised the Disease Outbreak Response System Condition (Dorscon) level to orange after several local cases without links to previous cases or travel history to China were tested positive. The orange level refers to a situation in which a virus is spreading but not widely. It involves introducing additional precautionary measures and enforcing compliance to contain the spread of the virus.

The next day, Prime Minister Lee Hsien Loong delivered a televised statement to alleviate fear and anxiety, urge Singaporeans to stay calm and carry on with their lives while taking sensible precautions, and rally the country to "take courage and see through this stressful time together." He highlighted that the ongoing virus outbreak is a test of Singapore's social cohesion and psychological resilience.

In my view, a key message in PM Lee's statement is the importance of psychological preparedness in our fight against the coronavirus.

Today is Singapore's Total Defence Day. Psychological defence is one of the six pillars of our total defence. What is the current state of our psychological defence against the virus threat?

BEING PSYCHOLOGICALLY PREPARED

In the past few days, daily updates from the Ministry of Health (MOH) reported more confirmed cases that do not have recent travel history or links to China. For the public, news of these local transmissions increases the salience of the virus threat. Understandably, many individuals begin to worry more about themselves, their family members and their friends.

At the media briefing on Wednesday, Health Minister Gan Kim Yong (chair of the Multi-Ministry Taskforce) cautioned that we have to be prepared for the worst as there could be patients who may succumb to the viral infection. This is psychologically important because a death is not just a fatality statistic — it also brings grief to families and friends, affects the morale of medical staff and front-line officers, and increases public fear, anxiety and other negative sentiments.

When it comes to test results, an increase in confirmed cases, recovery and death, we should hope for the best and be prepared for the worst. But psychological resilience is much more than our state of mind as we wait and react to daily updates from MOH.

At the same media briefing, National Development Minister Lawrence Wong (co-chair of the taskforce) acknowledged that the authorities do not know what sort of situation is going to unfold over the next few weeks and whether it will get better or worse.

Put in another way, we are currently in a VUCA situation — one that is volatile, uncertain, complex and ambiguous. But we need not be paralysed by the VUCA situation facing us. As individuals and in groups, we can make a positive difference not only to our lived experiences as the situation evolves but also to the type of society that we will become for years to come.

As the virus threat continues to loom, we need to understand psychological defence and shore it up at both the individual and societal levels.

PSYCHOLOGICAL CAPITAL

Individuals, organisations and communities need to develop "psychological capital", which provides the building blocks for our psychological defence. Psychological capital is a critical resource for individuals, and society collectively, to solve problems and improve well-being.

Research has shown that four interrelated mindsets — self-efficacy, optimism, hope and resilience — contribute to psychological capital that helps people function in adaptive ways, such as adjusting our lifestyle to take precautions and deal with the various control measures.

Psychological capital can be cultivated through training and education such as clearly explaining what we know and do not know about the coronavirus, what Dorscon risk assessment levels mean and entail, and the rationale for various precautionary measures and public health advisories.

Psychological capital can also be developed through real-life experiences such as working together to solve a problem, being involved in volunteer activities and providing social support to help those in need.

Psychological capital can become a powerful resource and motivation, characterised by a "can-do" spirit and a "will-do" attitude. We need to pay more attention to self-efficacy, optimism, hope and resilience as individuals adjust to the virus outbreak evolving in a VUCA situation.

PRINCIPLES TO GUIDE BEHAVIOURS

Psychological capital is an action-oriented resource. It produces positive behaviours. The resulting positive outcomes in turn reinforce the development of psychological capital.

There are many positive behaviours that we should or could engage in as we face the evolving virus outbreak situation. I suggest five principles to guide our behaviours.

Be Calm

We are likely to get more local transmissions in the coming days and weeks, with breaking news of new confirmed cases leading to disruptions in schools or workplaces. Some cases could be close to home — both physically and figuratively — as cases emerge near where we live, study or work, or when they directly affect our family, friends or colleagues. When that happens, our fear and anxiety levels will naturally rise. We immediately message one another to express our emotions and reactions.

How do we deal with this? Learn to take a deep breath, pause and reflect. Control our impulse to blame individuals, groups, organisations or the efficacy of containment measures before finding out the facts. No one wants to be infected or to infect others. With the virus circulating in our population, it is still possible to have an infected case even when sensible precautions are taken.

Being calm should not be confused with behaving in a nonchalant or overconfident manner, which is a negative attitude showing that one is not interested and does not care, downplaying the severity or trivialising the concerns expressed by others who perceive a serious virus threat.

Be Cautious

By now, everyone is familiar with the basic precautions. Practising good personal hygiene habits is the most important behaviour that each of us can do for ourselves and others. Instead of seeing it as an inconvenience, we should make it a habit to practise good personal hygiene behaviours for our own health and also out of social responsibility for public health.

The authorities are clearly working very hard to enhance the containment strategy and tighten the various control measures. At schools and workplaces, employers have to make quick decisions and often with incomplete information. Employees have to put up with inconveniences ranging from minor to major adjustments. But it can take just one careless individual to breach the control measures for an infection case and cluster to occur. We should be cautious and conscientious in adhering to the control measures in place.

Be Considerate

Fear and anxiety can override rationality and social norms, driving us to do things that we normally will not do or imagine ever doing. Last week, there was panic buying at supermarkets when the Dorscon level was raised to orange. We should be well-informed and inform others — it is a verifiable fact that Singapore has sufficient supplies of essential food items and an adequate food security system, with diversification of food sources so that there is enough food for everyone.

It is understandable and reasonable to buy a little more than usual if we plan to stay at home more in view of the virus outbreak. We should not "demonise" these people who are buying more out of necessity or reasonable convenience. But there is no need to hoard essential groceries and create our own stockpiles. We should be considerate and not deprive others who may be more in need of the items.

Another inconsiderate behaviour is depriving others of seats at the hawker centre or refusing to share common spaces out of fear of potential infection.

Being considerate to others is essentially civic minded-ness. It also applies to maintaining public hygiene such as keeping public places clean after use.

Be Caring

In crisis situations, it is important to care for others who are in need. The needs and care could be tangible such as distributing masks or hand sanitisers to those who need them and delivering meals or other items to those who have to stay at home to observe mandated leave of absence from work to monitor their health. Then there are intan-gible needs and care such as providing social support such as expressing gratitude and encouragement to our health-care workers, Home Team officers, cleaners and many others who are at the front line working to keep all of us safe.

Our medical workers and other front-line officers are putting in long hours under extremely challenging condi-tions. Without their courage and perseverance, we would be in a much more dire situation now. To stay the course, what they need from us is our social support, not social ostracism.

When our espoused values of care and compassion for others translate to actual value-driven behaviours, espe-cially in crisis situations where others are most in need of help and support, it becomes truly value-in-action.

Be Collectivistic

It is human that fear and anxiety for one's own health will automatically trigger self-preservation behaviours. But humans are also social beings interdependent on one another, capable of altruistic actions rooted in collectivistic values that go beyond individualistic interests.

Collectivism is a personal and social value that emphasises the interests and well-being of the larger group that we are a member of. It prioritises the group's concerns over one's own individual needs and desires. This larger group could be our neighbourhood, school, work organisation and, of course, country.

When we are collectivistic, we value and prioritise social cohesion. We see the strengths of working together in a coordinated, cooperative and collaborative way to achieve collective goals for the common good. Being collectivistic is critical in our battle against the virus outbreak.

CONCLUSION

Psychological capital and guiding principles are mutually reinforcing. For example, when people are optimistic and have the efficacy beliefs that they can make a positive difference to the morale of healthcare workers in difficult times, they are more likely to care and offer social support. Conversely, collectivistic behaviours guided by commitment to collective goals and trust developed from working together help build resilience in individuals as they persevere and learn to cope with difficult changes and adapt to new demands.

We need to shore up our psychological defence considerably and now, if we are to have a good chance of

Singapore seeing through this crisis. Focus on self-efficacy, optimism, hope and resilience to build psychological capital. A society with strong psychological capital can defuse an adverse climate and mitigate the impact of negative events and severe crises. It helps prevent negativity and promote positivity.

Along with building psychological capital, adopt the 5C principles of being calm, cautious, considerate, caring and collectivistic to guide our behaviours, so we make a positive difference. When we do that, we develop robust psychological defence. Then we can be realistically confident that we will defeat our public enemy, the coronavirus, and emerge stronger as individuals and as a society.

Chapter 14

Drill into What Makes People Socially Responsible

Singapore recently announced the setting up of an SG Clean Taskforce in its fight against the coronavirus, to get individuals and businesses to adopt good hygiene habits, keep public spaces clean, adjust social norms and behave in socially responsible ways.

The new taskforce has a dual challenge. It needs to effect changes quickly so that they become the first line of defence in the ongoing battle against COVID-19. It also needs to do it in ways that will develop permanent good habits and norms beyond the current outbreak.

Earlier this week, Health Minister Gan Kim Yong, who chairs the Multi-Ministry Taskforce on tackling COVID-19, reiterated the importance of social responsibility. He detailed how many locally transmitted cases were caused by individuals going to work, attending social activities and failing to minimise social contact even when they have flu-like symptoms such as cough and fever.

To deal with the outbreak requires not only a united response, but we also need to understand why people think, feel and act the way they do. Specifically, we need to drill down to what makes people behave responsibly socially, so we can find ways to encourage more of this and discourage socially irresponsible forms of behaviour.

BEING SOCIALLY RESPONSIBLE

It is not surprising that there are individuals in the community who are unwell but still perform daily routines or participate in group activities with unconstrained social interactions. They risk infecting others and sparking a chain of transmissions that can spiral out of control.

It is natural to feel angry and frustrated with these individuals because we see them as socially irresponsible, putting their selfish preferences above public health and the well-being of others. They cancel and reverse the positive effects of the control measures put in place.

Why do some people still persist in behaviours that are irresponsible to others?

Perhaps some are ignorant, complacent or overconfident. But psychology also tells us that people tend to underplay their symptoms or illness and their own risk of infection when there is an event they want to attend. This is even if they know that many people with COVID-19 had only mild symptoms but were already infectious.

Then there are those with prolonged flu-like symptoms who refuse to see the doctor because they fear being stigmatised if they were to test positive for COVID-19. Sadly, this fear is not without basis.

To deal with stigmatisation and discrimination, we need effective public education to create awareness that anyone can get infected, develop empathy for those infected, and understand that people with the infection discharged from hospitals in Singapore are fully recovered and no longer infectious.

Understanding the psychology behind their actions may explain why an individual decides to do or not do something. It does not justify or condone the socially irresponsible behaviour. No one has the right to expose others to the risk of illness just because he himself is not worried about getting sick — a person may be cavalier about his own health but must not assume others will feel likewise. Similarly, fear of stigmatisation does not give a person the right to mask his own symptoms and thus to expose many others to risks of illness and harm. These are socially irresponsible forms of behaviour.

We have seen from COVID-19 infections worldwide, especially in China and now in Italy, that the danger of widespread community transmission is real. In other words, infecting someone when going out sick is not a theoretical possibility. Rather, that action carries a certainty of exposing many people to the risk of falling ill unnecessarily, with a real chance of creating a chain of infections and severe negative consequences — all stemming from a personal decision or action.

When deciding whether or not to attend an event, or whether to proceed, cancel or postpone it, we should anticipate the negative consequences and the regret we will experience when they happen.

Health experts say that if many people get infected with COVID-19, hospitals can't cope with the sudden spike of cases. When this happens, some patients won't get the care they need and may die. It is as severe as that. This has already happened in China's Wuhan and in Italy, where doctors are rationing the use of ventilators that help sick patients breathe.

Once we understand the stakes involved and the moral choices we are making, we can see that social responsibility is also a test of our character, on whether we will do the right thing. Put in another way, social responsibility is not just about what we do to others but also who we truly are.

THE VINCE MODEL

To make people more socially responsible, we need to understand what factors affect behaviours. Based on research evidence, I have put together a five-factor model to help us understand the key drivers of behaviours and how they can be used to promote positive attitudes and change behaviours. I call it the VINCE model, referring to the five factors, namely values, image, norms, convenience and enforcement.

Values

Values are our convictions of what is important and they remind us of what ought to be. They shape our attitudes, thoughts, emotions and actions.

We can increase positive behaviours by reinforcing how they are consistent with our values. We can also decrease negative behaviours by highlighting how they are value-inconsistent. In this way, we can promote socially responsible behaviours and prevent socially irresponsible ones.

For example, social responsibility is based on care and concern for others, rooted in collectivistic values that prioritise the interests and well-being of the larger group (such as our work or social group) over our own individual needs and desires.

So, if we truly believe in these collectivistic values, then we should put the group interests before our self-interests. This means we do not participate in a group event when we are unwell even though we have an individual interest to attend. If we continue to attend, then our action is inconsistent with our espoused collectivistic values.

To build a culture of social responsibility in Singapore, we should develop and reinforce collectivistic values as our shared values.

Image

Image refers to how we see ourselves and how others see us.

It is human to want to have a positive self- and public image. It is adaptive when our self-image and public image match up and they reflect the reality of who we are and how others see us.

Self-image is made up of our beliefs and feelings about our characteristics as a person. For example, I may believe that I am a socially responsible person and I may feel good being one. Our beliefs and feelings are strengthened when we engage in actual behaviours widely considered to reflect the person characteristic.

Possible self-images and public images are powerful motivators for behaviour changes. When we are clear that hygiene behaviours affect the image of whether a person is socially responsible or irresponsible, we will put in effort to keep public places clean and adopt good hygiene habits, anticipating the positive images of a socially responsible person that we want to have and the negative images of a socially irresponsible person that we do not want.

Norms

Norms are cultural standards and social expectations shared by members of a community or society about what behaviours are appropriate or inappropriate in a given situation.

For example, we expect able-bodied individuals to give up their seats in trains to those who need them more. When entering or exiting a room, it is polite to hold the door open for the stranger immediately after you. Colleagues lunching together take turns to pay for the meals because of our norms of reciprocity.

Once established in a community, norms become social conventions of behaviours that are self-sustained. Members of the community follow social norms because they have internalised the normative rules of how to behave.

It is socially undesirable to deviate from norms. In any case people often do not deviate because the normatively appropriate behaviours have become habits that are somewhat automatic, reflex social actions in a situation.

For good hygiene behaviours to become habits, we need to cultivate cleanliness norms so that it is socially expected for everyone to keep public places clean.

A good normative principle to promote is that we should personally clean up a public place after using it so that it as clean or cleaner than just before we used it.

Convenience

Convenience refers to conditions that make it easier to do something without having to put in tedious effort. Research and anecdotal evidence have shown that a change in behaviour is more likely if the new behaviour is convenient to perform.

Two key features of convenience are availability and accessibility. That is why hawker centre patrons are more likely to return their food trays after eating if the location of the tray station is highly visible and easy to get to.

To enhance public hygiene and social responsibility, we need to make available and accessible to all individuals the relevant items, including soap in public toilets, sanitisers, thermometers and masks.

The authorities, organisations and organisers should also implement control measures in a simple way that will reduce unnecessary inconvenience and make it easy for people to comply. This is especially when some measures may be here to stay.

It could be something as simple as the way a travel declaration form is designed, the way a contact-tracing question is framed, the procedure for an employee to call in sick, or the ease for a patient to see the same clinic doctor again if he is still unwell or his medical certificate (MC) is expiring.

Enforcement

Enforcement is about ensuring compliance with rules and regulations, through monitoring, use of sanctions and other means. Examples of our current control measures for COVID-19 involving enforcement and compliance are travel restrictions, border controls, contact tracing, activity mapping, stay-home notices and quarantine orders.

We need to be socially responsible and comply with these measures strictly. For example, employers and employees must ensure that a worker who is unwell see a doctor promptly, even when symptoms are mild. The sick person must comply with the MC regime. It is critical to stay at home and not move around in the community so as to reduce the risk of community transmission, even when the individual "feels healthy".

Employers and colleagues must not exert pressure on the individual, directly or indirectly, to cause him to choose not to call in sick or quietly come back to work while unwell or on sick leave because he feels that work duty and obligation should take precedence.

Our control measures are time-sensitive, data-driven and resource-intensive. Socially irresponsible forms of behaviour, such as failing to cooperate, providing false information or breach in compliance, add an unnecessary significant load to our systems and workers and create problems that can have serious negative effects on containment of the outbreak and health outcomes. That is why such socially irresponsible forms of behaviour should be dealt with firmly and swiftly.

For enforcement to be effective, the authorities and employers need to implement rules and regulations that are practical and communicate them clearly, including what to do and what not to do. People must also know that enforcement is applied equally to all without fear or favour, and what the consequences of non-compliance are.

To conclude, we need to do much more to enhance hygiene habits and, more fundamentally, social responsibility.

It is natural to be angry and complain about people who are socially irresponsible. But each of us can galvanise others into taking positive actions.

Start first with ourselves and ensure that we personally practise what we preach about social responsibility. Be a role model to others and a positive influence for our family, friends and colleagues. Use the different factors in the Vince model to change attitudes and actions.

Chapter 15

A Toolkit to Deal with Negative Reactions in the COVID-19 Crisis

On Tuesday, when Singapore was midpoint in the four-week COVID-19 circuit breaker meant to last until May 4 to stem the spread of the coronavirus, Prime Minister Lee Hsien Loong announced the extension of the period by another four weeks to June 1.

Existing measures were also further tightened. Entry restrictions to hot spot areas such as popular wet markets were put in place to control crowding. The number of businesses deemed essential services and allowed to operate was cut.

The extension of the measures aims to minimise people movement and prevent mingling in the community. One key reason was that the daily number of unlinked cases — infections that cannot be traced to previous cases — did not decline even after two weeks of the circuit breaker, indicating the continual presence of undetected cases in the community.

Naturally, people are disappointed that the circuit breaker has to be extended. The coronavirus situation has also produced various negative reactions that both leaders and people themselves have to deal with. In this essay, I will share some suggestions on how to handle negative reactions and avoid the pitfalls produced by our human biases.

VARIETIES OF NEGATIVE REACTIONS

The tightening of the circuit breaker measures would have dismayed and inconvenienced many, even though support packages for businesses and workers will be extended through next month.

Those isolated at home or in their dormitories will find it increasingly difficult to cope — psychologically and in their daily functioning.

For example, working from home through telecommuting saves commuting time but may also create tension between work and personal or family life when individuals are unable to juggle competing demands now occurring in the same physical location (home) and time period.

Working parents with young children in particular may find it difficult to balance working from home and having to attend to children's needs given that schools and childcare facilities are closed.

It also becomes more challenging if demanding supervisors expect their subordinates to attend online meetings and work outside their normal working hours. Those in positions of power need to be more respectful of the people they lead and not encroach on hours after work.

In addition to having to multitask and deal with competing demands, dealing with a pandemic like COVID-19 is already a stressful experience that can readily generate negative emotions or reactions.

People may experience fear (Will I get infected?), anxiety (Will my business survive the extended circuit breaker?), hopelessness (We will never recover), loneliness (There is no one that I can turn to), confusion (Is it better to wear or not wear a mask when I am jogging outside?), anger (This violation of the safe distancing rule is unacceptable!), feelings of injustice (This differential treatment of the two violations is unfair — it's double standards) or even denial and engage in bargaining behaviours (Can I just not wear the mask for this one time?) or withdrawal behaviours (I don't care anymore).

For some individuals, boredom, feelings of injustice or self-centred interests will override their sensibility and sense of social responsibility, and they will violate circuit breaker measures (either negligently or knowingly) or even influence others to do likewise.

Negative emotions can easily get magnified. They can create a negative spiral that gets out of control and proportion when we do not recognise that the feelings are driving our attitudes and actions, do nothing to address them or reinforce the feelings by engaging only with others who share the same sentiments.

All of us need to learn now how to deal with negative reactions and mitigate their impact, especially when it is possible that the COVID-19 crisis will get worse.

ADOPT THE 3Rs APPROACH

How then to respond effectively to deal with negative events and manage our negative gut emotions and reactions? I suggest we adopt what I call the 3Rs approach — refrain, reflect and resolve.

Refrain

Refrain means to control the impulse to immediately argue, advocate or act in a way that is driven by how we are feeling at the moment.

It worsens the situation when others are also consumed with emotions and not thinking rationally. Never react in a patronising or provocative manner — it will only intensify the experience of our negative emotion. For example, if someone in line is standing too close to you, gently gesture to the person to the safe distancing marking on the floor, and do so with a smile.

More generally, when dealing with disagreement, be composed, not confrontational. It helps to be calm and cordial. Ask questions to clarify and ascertain facts.

Treat others with dignity and respect, and they will become more reasonable, and more likely to focus on the positives than magnify the negatives.

Reflect

Think through and identify the information or event, and the sources of our stress and strain.

Learn to see things from another's perspective. Reflect on how things have come to this situation where we have to deal with negative events and why we are reacting negatively. This often involves reinterpreting the situation because we tend to first interpret things in a way to fit our beliefs and position.

Rather than see the prolonged circuit breaker period as a nuisance, we can reframe the experience as an opportunity to take control of our diet or learn a new skill. We may want to relook our business model, consider a job switch, rearrange work priorities or revisit career goals.

Make an effort to gather information from multiple sources and try to be objective. Consult others who have expertise, especially those who can be trusted to tell the truth and provide sincere advice. Identify and acknowledge the mistakes we may have made.

Resolve

Take concrete actions to reduce damage and stressors, repair relationships and resolve issues. Be humble and seek help when needed.

When there are disagreements, focus on common and complementary interests, even if differences remain.

So, when negotiating work-related arrangements to adjust to the circuit breaker measures, both employers and employees need to aim for win-win outcomes. This often involves being gracious and generous in spirit, without compromising facts, truth and integrity.

When an issue is successfully resolved, learn from the experience and identify relevant features of the solution process to adapt and apply to other situations or future ones.

NEGATIVE REACTIONS AND LEADERSHIP

In a crisis, people must learn to deal with their negative emotions, and leaders too need to manage these public reactions. But how people react is also influenced by their leaders' attitudes and actions.

So, leaders in all sectors and at all levels need to understand how negative reactions emerge and how they relate to the major types of human cognitive biases. They should self-reflect regularly to avoid themselves falling prey to these biases when they make decisions and judgement calls.

I have previously written on various well-established human biases. Let me reiterate three types of biases that we need to guard against in this circuit breaker period.

Overconfidence Bias

Overconfidence is ubiquitous when humans make judgments and decisions. Most people are also overconfident about the accuracy of their forecasts.

There is a substantial gap between what people think they know and what they actually know.

Research shows that this disconnect between self-belief and reality is larger for people with higher academic achievements, experts in various fields, and those in positions of authority and power.

Confirmatory Bias

Confirmatory bias is the human tendency to selectively seek out and interpret information in a way that will likely confirm one's preconceived belief or position. We see what we expect to see.

The same decision, event, statement or data can mean something very different to different individuals or groups.

The problem of confirmatory bias gets more severe if the authority structure and dynamics in the policy team encourage groupthink, where members of a highly cohesive group withhold dissenting views to go along with majority opinion. Many misunderstandings and incorrect conclusions could have been avoided if decision makers had asked: "What else could it mean?"

Causal Attribution Bias

When we try to understand or explain why we do well, we tend to attribute our own successes to internal factors such as our own ability, effort, plans, choices or judgments.

But we tend to attribute our failures to external factors — we say bad luck, the task is difficult, the problem is complex, or the situation has changed.

And when we make causal attributions about others, we tend to do the reverse — we see external factors in their successes and internal factors in their failures.

That is why public perceptions often differ significantly from leaders' perceptions. Consider, for example, the spike in COVID-19 cases among foreign workers in the dormitories. Leaders may say this is due to a rapidly evolving situation that is uncertain, complex and volatile.

But the public — especially when they do not have relevant information or understand trade-offs involved — is more likely to attribute the negative outcome to the leaders' problem-solving ability, believing that they were careless or incompetent.

Conversely, leaders may choose to credit a serendipitous or positive outcome to good policy design and execution. But the public is more likely to attribute it to luck, or to take the view that a leader with ample resources should be expected to produce such results.

MOVING FORWARD

Since the beginning of the coronavirus outbreak, Singapore has rightly emphasised that what is at stake are people's lives and livelihood, that people's well-being must be at the centre of what we do in managing the crisis.

We can be realistically confident that we will defeat the coronavirus if we are self-disciplined and socially responsible, and if we find our leaders trustworthy.

Our trust in leaders increases if they are able to solve urgent practical problems, say what they mean and mean what they say, are objective, transparent, fair and accountable when they make judgements and decisions, and understand, empathise with and prioritise the people's needs and concerns.

Also, regardless of who we are, we need to better understand why people react the way they do, and how to deal with negative emotions and experiences. This affects our adaptability and resilience as individuals, families, organisations and a society.

When we understand people's perceptions and reactions, we will all be more psychologically prepared to face the COVID-19 crisis and its great disruptions, both now and in the future.

Chapter 16

How to Make Critical Decisions Amid COVID-19 Pressures

The COVID-19 crisis has affected people's quality of life and livelihoods, and it will continue to do so. There are many new demands to adapt to, both ongoing ones and those in the post-pandemic realities.

Amid adaptation challenges galore, we sometimes have to make decisions involving high stakes, under time and conflicting pressures.

The stakes are high because the decisions have important implications for ourselves, our loved ones or even our nation.

Pressures abound when we need to decide one way or the other within a short time, and it is unclear to us which is best or better.

Consider some examples under COVID-19 pressures: Should I switch or stay in my job? Should I close or continue my business? Should I spend the money now or save it for future needs? Should I vote for A or B in this election?

Depending on the choices available, our experiences and the prevailing circumstances and the possible futures, deciding to go one way may be better than the other.

These factors are different for different individuals, so there is no science that can tell us which decision is better. But behavioural sciences can help us make better decisions by understanding the factors that go into making decisions in difficult times.

TIME PRESSURE

Behavioural sciences tell us that time pressure occurs when we have less time available than we think we need to come to a decision.

Research has shown how time pressure affects the way we think and feel, which in turn influence our decision-making process.

First, when we are under time pressure, we tend to narrow our cognitive focus. We zero in to think about one or two issues that we consider relevant and key, and then proceed to come to a decision.

We are less likely to brainstorm ideas, identify possibilities, seek feedback or advice, and consider different viewpoints.

The problem of narrow focus is not just insufficient scope. It is exacerbated by confirmatory bias — our human tendency to selectively seek out and interpret information in a way that will likely confirm our preconceived belief about a particular option. This could be either a positive or negative evaluation of the option.

The consequence is that we see what we expect to see, which in turn strengthen our belief or position, never mind what the objective facts are.

Next, time pressure not only produces stress but also a variety of emotions. For instance, we may feel angry or cynical or develop a sense of unfairness if we think that the issue is too important to be decided in the short time given, or that the decision-making time span imposed is unnecessarily short.

It is important to know that time pressures can easily evoke these negative emotions. Such negative feelings can influence our decision-making more than it should or we want to let them, and therefore bias our decision without us knowing it.

This applies even when it is understandable or justifiable to feel negative about the time pressure.

For example, when asked to decide to accept or reject a job offer, it is understandable that we feel negative if we are given a shorter deadline than we like.

But even if the short deadline is a relevant consideration, we should not let our negative feelings about it disproportionately influence our evaluation of the job offer and end up not examining those factors that are important when making the decision.

Typically, time pressure does not generate positive emotions, but it can still tilt us to favour a particular option when we feel the need to make a decision quickly.

This happens because of the halo effect and the optimism bias.

The halo effect occurs when we have a positive overall or first impression of a person or product, and it leads us to conclude positive things about other distinct aspects even though we do not have the relevant information to make a proper evaluation.

For example, we may conclude that a person who came from a humble background is also an honest person, even though we have no factual information about the person's honesty. There is no evidence that socio-economic status and honesty are correlated.

The halo effect becomes more problematic if our positive overall or first impression is misguided, or if it was previously valid but is no longer so.

The halo effect can thus lead to inflated positive evaluation of an option, and also result in our missing negative characteristics that might have affected our decision had we considered them.

A preferred option already burnished by the halo effect may be strengthened further by confirmatory bias or optimism bias. That is, being overconfident of our own judgements and having an unrealistic belief that the future will be better, even though there is no supporting evidence.

AMBIVALENCE PRESSURES

Apart from encountering time pressure, anyone making decisions in a crisis may also experience feelings of ambivalence.

We may be torn between A and B because we have mixed feelings about either choice.

This is no different from many aspects in our personal lives or at work. We both like and dislike certain traits of our spouse, friend, colleague or boss. We have both positive and negative feelings about working from home. We feel conflicted when put in a moral-dilemma situation.

We have mixed feelings and thoughts when reacting to major policy debates on controversial issues.

The experience of mixed feelings and thoughts, or what psychologists call "ambivalence", is a state of internal conflict.

Due to the COVID-19 crisis, ambivalence pressures are particularly salient and stressful for people when the stakes are high, such as deciding whether to change jobs or whether to close or continue a business that is badly bruised.

We recognise there are pros and cons, but we are unable, or find it very difficult, to choose between two opposing options or actions to arrive at a decision.

When we are in a state of ambivalence, we feel conflicted because we have beliefs or experience emotions that are incompatible.

Conflicts of belief occur because we need our thoughts to be coherent when we form judgments about a same person or group — we want our various beliefs to be internally consistent.

We see positive traits as consistent with one another but not with negative traits, and conversely, we see the same for negative traits. Which is why seeing a mix of positive and negative traits in the same person or group leads to ambivalence in beliefs about the person or group.

Emotional conflict is felt most when we experience incompatible emotions — love and anger towards someone we care about, or respect for and disappointment with the leaders we support.

For example, we experience strong emotional conflicts when we have to decide whether to report a wrongdoing committed by a close friend or someone we look up to. We are torn between feelings of loyalty to friendship or mentorship, and feelings of responsibility to the organisation or society.

When we experience belief or emotional conflict, our dissonance and feelings dominate. They can easily overwhelm and override the rational reasoning that we may engage in initially. Moreover, being pulled in two opposite directions is psychologically discomforting.

That is why when we experience ambivalence from having strong opposing beliefs or incompatible emotions, we feel pressured to quickly take a position and reinforce that position, especially when we think we need to make a decision soon.

But rushing to a decision makes us susceptible to cognitive biases and emotion-based influences. We become more vulnerable to confirmatory bias, halo effect, optimism bias and strategic persuasion by others.

To avoid making a decision prematurely because of ambivalence pressures, we need to pause and think about the future consequences of a decision.

Relate the consequences to what really matters to us, anticipate the regret we will feel from not thinking through before deciding, and focus on the benefits we can have from making the effort to arrive at a decision.

This is easier said than done. We need some practical guidance to do this.

GETTING BETTER AT MAKING DECISIONS

To resolve ambivalence while under time pressure to make a decision, we should focus on four areas.

Goals

When under time pressure and conflicted by competing beliefs and opposing emotions, ask what the goals that we really want to achieve are.

When goals are clarified, some of the positives and negatives in the mix may change in their relevance and impact.

Also consider how goals are related to one another. If the goals are contradictory, we need to prioritise, coordinate, choose or make trade-offs. But if they are common, or at least not mutually exclusive, we can connect them to converge with or complement one another.

Insights

Learn and apply the insights on time pressure and ambivalence. This involves evaluating our beliefs and regulating our emotions. Be aware of our own biases.

We gain new insights when we examine issues in context and find out facts objectively, instead of seeking out information selectively to confirm beliefs.

Check with those who can be trusted to tell the truth. Consult those who are knowledgeable in the relevant area, especially when the time available to make a decision is limited.

Values

Values represent our convictions of what is important and remind us of what ought to be. They shape our attitudes, affect our thoughts, influence our emotions and guide our behaviours.

Values are critical when we are emotionally conflicted. Our emotions may contest our rationality. But our emotions are often influenced by our values, and can change to align with our value system.

To respond to time pressure and resolve ambivalence, put our core values at the centre of what we think and feel, and how we act.

This could mean cherishing character traits of integrity and accountability, creating a fair and just society, or caring about our country and our fellow citizens.

Expectations

Evaluate whether what we hope to happen, and believe can happen, are based on realistic expectations and therefore is likely to happen.

When expectations are realistic, they are also less likely to be extremely positive or negative. This in turn reduces the intensity of ambivalence.

When presented with arguments on what might happen if we choose one way as opposed to the other, distinguish between what is possible merely in theory, and what is practical and more plausible.

When under time pressure, search for relevant information and verify facts to engender more realistic and well-informed expectations.

To conclude, adopt the "GIVE" approach to clarify our goals, capitalise on the insights, centre on our values, and calibrate our expectations.

The COVID-19 crisis creates new high-stakes decision-making demands on us, with time and ambivalent pressures. No one can dictate to us which decision is best, nor can science prescribe the answer. But we can become better at making decisions.

Chapter 17

Foster Positivity Amid COVID-19 Challenges

Like many societies, Singapore has seen its people stepping up to help the needy during the COVID-19 crisis, volunteering, donating and raising funds for vulnerable groups such as migrant workers, lower-income families and people who have lost their jobs. Businesses, too, give back to the community through donations of cash, masks, sanitisers, food and other essential items.

These helping behaviours complement the Government's efforts to reach out to needy individuals and families. This is critical, given the urgent needs and the scale and speed of the economic, social and psychological impact from COVID-19 challenges.

Equally important, the voluntary acts of giving reflect and reinforce the positive attitudes and experiences of the people and the community amid the COVID-19 global pandemic. This positivity occurs for both the giver and the recipient, and it has multiplier effects.

Positivity also contributes to Singapore's psychological defence in the fight against the coronavirus by helping to build the psychological capital that people need, to adapt and deal with the multiple challenges — self-efficacy, optimism, hope, resilience.

Even though Singapore has lifted the circuit breaker and we are gradually reopening the economy, many individuals and families hit severely by the COVID-19 crisis will continue to experience hardship or distress. Moreover, when new waves of infection hit, restrictive curbs may kick in again, resulting in new or exacerbated needs.

Positive attitudes and experiences help people deal with adaptation challenges associated with strict containment measures and post-pandemic realities. They also help with learning and adaptability when people have to leave their comfort zone to pick up new skills by attending training or take up a traineeship opportunity as a transit to a permanent job.

To increase our psychological preparedness and adaptability, we need to understand the science of positivity.

POSITIVE PSYCHOLOGY OF GIVING

An aspect of positivity that is important for tackling COVID-19 challenges is subjective well-being, which is about satisfaction and happiness. Such subjective well-being is important in helping individuals cope better.

Let's drill into the components of subjective well-being. Satisfaction is the extent to which we evaluate that our needs, wants and preferences are met. It is the cognitive component of subjective well-being.

Happiness is the extent of positive emotions we are experiencing, such as a personal sense of meaning or feelings of joy. It is the emotional component.

Together, satisfaction and happiness help us understand how people evaluate and experience their lives.

Giving creates positive well-being because recipients' needs are satisfied, and givers experience positive emotions when they see their deeds benefit other who need help. The positive attitudes and experiences are mutually reinforcing between the givers and the recipients of help.

Research has shown that giving time, money and other assistance not only benefits the recipient but also leads to positive outcomes for the giver. When people give, they derive a sense of personal meaning from helping others. They also better appreciate their own circumstances as they learn of the situations facing the less fortunate.

The interaction between the givers and the recipients also produces positive social relationships and builds social capital that will benefit the community in many ways.

In the challenging times of the protracted COVID-19 crisis, it is even more important to foster such positivity. One way to do this is to involve people in giving such as donation, volunteerism, and other community work.

MEANING AND GROWTH NEEDS

Another type of positivity revolves around meaning and growth needs. Meeting such needs motivates positive behaviours. They enable positive attitudes and experiences at work.

Positivity at work can be encouraged when we develop certain core job characteristics that generate meaning and growth.

For example, are we creating and nurturing job characteristics and work conditions for people to want to learn new skills and apply them, and also for people to enjoy what they do at work?

Studies have shown that job characteristics such as skill variety, task identity and task significance are motivating for most employees, and they lead to positive attitudes and behaviours at work.

Skill variety lets us use and practise the different skills that we have. Task identity means we can identify with what we do as being responsible for the whole or more complete outcome of the work. Task significance means we can see that what we do contributes to something wider beyond ourselves such as the organisation or society.

Two extra job characteristics or work conditions matter to many people — having a reasonable level of autonomy or freedom to decide how to accomplish our task and the opportunity to receive feedback to know how effective we are at work.

Together, the above five job characteristics help make work more meaningful, make us feel responsible for work outcomes, and help us see the results of our work. These experiences lead to positive work-related outcomes such as better job performance, higher job satisfaction, and more organisational citizenship behaviours.

As we navigate harsh post-pandemic realities involving disruptive changes in jobs and work processes, it is important to attend to these job characteristics to motivate positive work behaviours and outcomes, and ensure that the personal sense of human dignity is developed and not diminished through work.

POSITIVITY CAN COUNTER NEGATIVITY

Research has shown that positivity can effectively counter negativity.

But first, negative emotion by itself is not the same as negativity. When our goals are frustrated, we experience negative emotions. Similarly, we feel negative when someone behaves in a way that impedes or hurts the progress towards a collective goal that we and many others are helping to achieve.

An example is when someone violates a COVID-19 safe management rule and behaves in a socially irresponsible way when most of us are adhering to the measures to contain the spread of the coronavirus. But that is not negativity — it is simply a negative reaction that we experience.

Negativity, in contrast, is a mindset, not just a momentary emotion or reaction. For example, negativity manifests itself when we form a negative opinion based on simply knowing who the person is or which group he or she belongs to, regardless of what the person says or does. When we consistently evaluate others negatively because of their particular group membership or who they are, such as being member of a political party or a nationality group, instead of what they said or did, it is a type of negative confirmatory bias which accumulates to form negativity.

Negativity is often developed, and strengthened over time, by repeated unresolved negative experiences and emotions. So, don't just lament or lambast negativity. Empathise with people's negative experiences, and seek to understand why things have come to this.

Positivity, however, is not the direct opposite of negativity — it is not a positive confirmatory bias. As I have explained previously, positivity involves positive attitudes and experiences such as self-efficacy and sense of meaning, and they lead to actual positive outcomes like performance and helping behaviour.

Research has shown that it is possible for us to become lower on negativity without, at the same time, becoming higher on positivity. Conversely, it is possible to be low on positivity without being high on negativity. So, a reduction in negativity by itself does not mean that positivity is increased, and vice versa.

But research has also shown that it is not quite possible to be consistently high in both positivity and negativity at the same time. The two are counteracting in that having high intensity on one — either positivity or negativity — will make it difficult to simultaneously have high intensity on the other. One can be low on both positivity and negativity, or high on either one but low on the other, but it is difficult to be high on both.

Taken together, the evidence indicates that positivity and negativity are not direct opposite poles of the same thing. They are different constructs that are inversely and moderately correlated.

So, while it may be difficult to directly reduce negativity, it is constructive to focus on increasing positivity. When we successfully increase positivity, we reduce negativity and therefore the negative outcomes associated with negativity.

Positivity is probably the most effective way to counter negativity. At the same time, we achieve the many direct benefits of positivity.

In managing negative reactions during the COVID-19 crisis, it is important to understand the distinction between negative emotions and negativity, and how positivity can effectively counter negativity.

Back to the example of public reactions to a violation of safe management practices. There have been numerous cases of people ignoring control measures and behaving irresponsibly, such as not wearing a face mask in public and failing to maintain social distancing. Photos of these violations were circulated in social media and also reported by mainstream media.

In all of these cases, regardless of the nationality of the offenders, Singaporeans experienced negative emotions and reacted angrily, and understandably so, because the offenders were socially irresponsible and frustrating our collective goals to curb the spread of the coronavirus in the community.

However, in those cases that involved offenders who are foreigners, some Singaporeans generalised their negative comments to foreigners in general living in Singapore or alleged that foreigners receive preferential favourable treatment in the enforcement of the COVID-19 safe management rules.

In commenting on the public reactions to these violations, policymakers and community leaders should not confuse or unwittingly give the impression that they have confused an important distinction. The legitimately negative emotion experienced by the general public when they reacted to the socially irresponsible behaviours of the offenders (regardless of their nationality) is not the same as the negativity that some Singaporeans manifest when they extrapolate negative sentiments to all foreigners in Singapore and make unfounded allegations about preferential treatment.

The first is an understandable negative reaction to a specific irresponsible act such as not wearing a mask. The second is a negativity mindset that has been built up towards foreigners, which need addressing.

But if we focus exclusively or disproportionately on calling out Singaporeans' negative comments on foreigners and labelling the reactions as xenophobic, then this dominant approach to managing negativity is counterproductive — it will just create more negativity because the public will rightly or wrongly perceive that their concerns and legitimate negative reactions are ignored or trivialised.

So, it is important to distinguish between negative emotions and negativity, and between negativity and positivity.

Public expressions of negative emotions need not always be a bad thing. They reflect people's concerns, aspirations, goals and experiences. They highlight the need to clarify facts, ensure impartiality, and enhance fairness perceptions. They can and have helped policymakers and leaders identify problems, revisit priorities and formulate solutions.

But, whoever we are, we can learn to respond appropriately to avoid unintended consequences that end up fostering more negativity.

Finally, let's focus more on fostering positivity in the community to address negativity and tackle COVID-19 adaptation challenges. Positivity is necessary for us to emerge stronger and better from the coronavirus crisis.

Chapter 18

The Psychology of Trust Amid COVID-19 Challenges

(This invited article first appeared in the 2021 Quarter 2 issue of the SID Directors Bulletin, published by the Singapore Institute of Directors).

To build a high-trust climate, leaders need to understand better how humans think, feel and act in the context of the issues that people care about. Why and how does the psychology of trust matter in navigating COVID-19 challenges?

The COVID-19 pandemic has caused and will continue to cause great disruption to lives, livelihoods, ways of life and quality of life. Yet, post the pandemic, daily functioning will not be the same. The immense, unexpected impact of COVID-19 has highlighted the urgency to restructure the way we live, work, learn and play, in anticipation of a future "Disease X" that could be more virulent and infectious.

To effectively function in the new normal, a principled, adaptive leadership in which leaders' decisions, words and actions are highly trusted by the public is needed. Trust is critical for problem-solving because a baseline level of trust is foundational for people to believe their leaders and decide to cooperate or be motivated to perform actions towards achieving the intended outcome.

When public trust is low, effective functioning is hampered — leaders, be they in governments, businesses or non-profit organisations, will find it extremely difficult to implement a control measure or an initiative, change a prior decision or explain the change, and galvanise people to collectively manage a crisis. Research in behavioural sciences has consistently shown that trust in leaders is difficult to build, easily eroded, and difficult to restore once lost.

In addition, leaders are susceptible to the same human biases of overconfidence and low self-awareness. Many leaders not only think they are better than they actually are, they also overestimate their followers' perception of their trustworthiness.

An evidence-based approach to building trust, that understands how humans think, feel and act in the context of the issues people care about, can help leaders prevent trust erosion, repair trust violation and enhance trust development.

For this to happen, it is important to have the humility, learning orientation and objectivity to draw lessons on trust in leadership. Singapore's responses and experiences in the COVID-19 crisis so far provide rich case examples of public trust issues.

To contextualise trust, we need to define the specific issue, situation and time period. A useful framework is what I call the 3Ms of trust matters, which looks at trust as Multi-level, Multi-dimensional and Malleable.

TRUST IS MULTI-LEVEL

Trust is multi-level. It is essential to recognise the different aspects of trust at different levels, from individual to group to institution.

Individual Level

The individual level is fundamental because trust is essentially a psychological construct, and it is really the perception of trust that matters. A trustee (e.g., the leader seeking to be trusted) may be objectively trustworthy on an issue, but if the trustor (e.g., the person deciding whether to trust the leader) does not perceive the trustee as trustworthy (because other factors such as coordination or communication have negatively affected the trust perception), there will still be low trust. The level of distrust matters because it affects how the trustor thinks, feels and acts, which, in turn, could lead to important individual and collective actions or reactions.

Group Level

Trust can also occur at the team or group level. Do you trust the 4G leaders (fourth generation of political leaders in Singapore)? When answering this question, you are thinking of the 4G as a team, as the abstract trustee, without necessarily thinking of any particular individual leader. But it may take just one individual leader in the team to behave in a certain way to increase or decrease your level of trust for the 4G as a team. This can also happen at the organisational level when we talk about the level of trust that an employee has in the senior management leadership team.

Inter-group Level

At the team or group level, we can examine inter-team trust or inter-group trust. In Singapore, we often talk about social cohesion and harmony in terms of trust between groups, such as between different racial groups or religious groups. Singapore needs to pay attention to other emergent group differences, such as trust between locals and foreigners, or between other emergent groups categorised according to variables like age or socio-economic class demographics, and even value beliefs or positions (such as attitudes towards LGBT [lesbian, gay, bisexual, and transgender] issues).

Inter-group trust is important for social cohesion. Without it, there would be wider social divides in the larger society in which the groups are a part. Inter-group trust is also critical to enable groups to work together and turn group differences into complementary strengths in diversity rather than conflicting weaknesses in disagreements. So, it is crucial to develop a climate of inter-group trust. For example, when creating public spaces and amenities or common facilities at the workplace, leaders should consider how this can be done to facilitate positive naturalistic interactions among diverse groups of people.

Institutional Level

There is also public trust at the level of institutions and the government. When we talk about public trust in Singapore, we often refer to trust in the Singapore Government and specific public institutions such as the enforcement agencies. Although this notion of public trust is clear in terms of the trustee, the issues are complex, such as which dimensions of trust are in question and how they are related. This brings us to the concept of multi-dimensionality, which is the second M of trust matters.

TRUST IS MULTI-DIMENSIONAL

Trust is multi-dimensional, for both parties (the trustor and the trustee) in a trust relationship.

Beliefs

A citizen's propensity to trust the government is affected by his or her personal beliefs and perceptions about the government. This subjectivity is only partly dependent on, and sometimes even independent of, the government's objective trustworthiness. This is because the government's objective trustworthiness is sometimes not evident to the citizen for various reasons.

For example, the citizen may lack access to relevant information. Alternatively, a failure in government coordination or public communication may have confounded the issues and led to a negative trust perception. Also, the citizen may have misinterpreted certain facts or been misled to believe that some falsehoods or inaccuracies are factually true.

Expectations

Trust also comes with the public having certain expectations, such as what the government and leaders will or will not do. For example, we expect leaders to have public consultations when designing or implementing certain policies, and we expect leaders to not omit important information when providing us facts to make our personal decisions. When this expectation is not met, it leads to negative emotions, perceptions or even retaliatory actions.

On the other side of the relationship, the trustee's trustworthiness as perceived by the trustor, is based on what the trustor thinks about the trustee's competence, integrity and benevolence.

Trust in Competence

Trust in competence refers to people's perception of the leader's ability to solve problems and effectively address their concerns. In the case of governments, this trust dimension refers to the public's confidence in national leaders and the governing bodies to perform and solve problems affecting people's lives, such as those relating to infrastructure, public transport, delivery of public services, and the effectiveness in managing crises.

Trust in Integrity

Trust in integrity has to do with the perception of the leader's character. It involves issues of honesty, incorruptibility and impartiality. The focus is on the integrity of the person (such as public service officers and political leaders), but it also involves the perception of how breaches of integrity are handled. In Singapore, the Government's vigorous actions against those caught for corruption, regardless of who they are, may mitigate the erosion of trust due to integrity breaches to some extent and reinforce the government's position on zero tolerance for such wrongdoings.

Trust in Benevolence

Trust in benevolence refers to public confidence that the leader or government is authentic (saying what it means and meaning what it says) and has good intentions or motivations when making a decision or undertaking a particular action or policy.

Trust in benevolence increases when people believe that the policy or government action is intended to serve their interests and is motivated by genuine concern for citizen well-being, rather than personal vested interests. It gets eroded when people think that policies and decisions affecting them are made by an elite who is disconnected from ground sentiments and is unable or unwilling to empathise with or does not care enough for the less fortunate and the ordinary folk.

Trust in benevolence is one of the hardest forms of trust to gain. It is one that means a lot to the public or followers, but is often neglected by leaders. Often, the problem may not be that the leadership is insincere, but that it is not perceived as sincere because it has not paid adequate attention to the nature of its actions, engagement and communications.

See BOX 1, "Trust, Engagement, Implementation" for how all the different dimensions of trust come into play in the issues related the TraceTogether contact tracing technology and privacy protection.

BOX 1: TRUST, ENGAGEMENT, IMPLEMENTATION

Public trust, public engagement and policy implementation are inter-related. Take, for example, the issues involved in the implementation of the TraceTogether contact tracing technology and privacy protection.

Public engagement should be clear on how privacy concerns are addressed. The explanation of the government's decisions should focus on the significant increase in speed and accuracy that these technologies and data collected offer in contact tracing when used to complement and supplement the human efforts and judgments of the contact tracers. The key point is this is not just a "good-to-have" add-on feature in contact tracing but a critical toolkit to save lives and livelihoods by protecting public health and preventing community transmission.

Privacy protection is more than an ideological debate. It is as much an issue of trust perception of the government's competence, integrity and benevolence.

If the government is well-coordinated across agencies; effective in its whole-of-government approach; prompt, open and transparent in its public communication; focused on individual well-being; shows humility and empathy in its public engagement efforts, then the TraceTogether adoption (usage) rate will increase substantially. This will, in turn, translate into the intended public health outcomes that benefit the people, and public trust in the leadership (competence, integrity, benevolence) will

---

BOX 1: (*Continued*)

increase as people observe the government's attitudes and actions and see the outcomes.

Conversely, if the government fails to uphold trust in competence, integrity and benevolence, then people will experience various negative emotions, from anger and anxiety to disappointment and frustration. They become cynical when reacting to new policies or announcements on new technology, and technological adoption rate will remain low. Even if made compulsory, people will find ways not to use it.

TRUST IS MALLEABLE

Trust is malleable, which simply means it can change. This may seem obvious, but many often fail to appreciate its implications.

Trust takes time to build, but it is easy to lose, and once lost, it is difficult to restore. The point is not to lament on the fragility of trust, but to understand what it means for trust building since trust can change.

Changes Over Time

The first step is to know that trust is dynamic and sensitive to the context. A trust level at any one point in time must never be taken as fixed or a given. The level of trust can change gradually or abruptly. It may increase or decrease depending on the prevailing factors that impact trust, thereby producing a pattern or change trajectory over time.

The dynamic nature of trust is why it is very difficult to predict future levels of public trust based on historical trends. For example, you could have trusted the government for the past 20 years, but if it does something now that really violates your values, you may stop trusting it.

Trust need not change gradually — it can move rapidly and abruptly, depending on changes in context. Therefore, leaders need to be careful when making decisions and policies based on trends and projections. Many leaders underestimate the overdependence on past trends. Trust levels in previous years may give the leader some relevant context and data reference. But what happens in the next year depends a lot on what the leaders do this year, and what the people perceive of their leaders.

Lived Experiences

The limitation of using past trends of trust levels to predict current and future levels of trust must not be confused with the separate issue of changes in people's lived experiences over time. The pattern of these changes is critical in influencing trust levels. When citizens go to vote at the ballot box or decide on how to respond to their leaders on an issue, they do not care where Singapore stands in a global ranking of country trust levels or how their organisations fared as compared to trust in other organisations. What they care about is where their well-being stands today as compared to the past few years of their lives.

It is the lived experiences that the people go through that will determine their trust levels and their reactions, in both their attitudes and actions. So, it is intra-individual, intra-country and intra-organisational changes in trust levels, and not inter-country or inter-organisation rankings, that are more and most important for leaders to bear in mind.

UNDERSTANDING, DEVELOPING AND MAINTAINING TRUST

In order to develop and maintain trust, we have to understand the science of trust and also translate it into practice. The key issues in the science and practice of trust may be summarised in the following areas:

- Assess the dimensionality of trust (competence, integrity, benevolence).
- Understand the content and context of trust, distrust (low trust), mistrust (trusting when should not).
- Monitor trust levels and dynamics (how trust evolves and changes over time).
- Deal with "trust-in-transition" (responding to feelings of doubt and ambivalence by the trustors towards the trustee. See BOX 2, "Trust-in-Transition Cases").
- Repair trust violation (how trust erodes and how to prevent it; how to restore and rebuild trust).
- Develop and increase trust (efficacy of approaches to enhance trust levels).
- Create and influence trust climate (shared perceptions of trust among a group or community of individuals).

Trust does not occur or change in a vacuum — the way leaders approach issues matters a great deal. See BOX 3, "Strategic Approaches to Develop Trust" for how governments and organisations and their leaders can develop trust with their stakeholders.

BOX 2: TRUST-IN-TRANSITION CASES

In the challenges concerning the migrant worker dormitory outbreak and TraceTogether technology, many of the issues relate to trust perceptions.

There were issues of trust in leadership competence with the rapid spike and sustained numbers of high daily confirmed COVID-19 cases in the dormitories. Questions were raised on how this could have occurred or could have been prevented or mitigated earlier.

In the use of TraceTogether technology for contact tracing, there were issues of trust (in competence, integrity, benevolence) related to the collection, storage and use of personal data. In June 2020, the Government had provided categorical assurance that the data collected by TraceTogether are used for and only for contact tracing of COVID-19. However, a ministerial response in Parliament in January 2021 said that the police is also authorised to access and use TraceTogether data for criminal investigation purposes, and had done so. This sparked a public debate and negative public perception.

The Government has since acknowledged that it made an error and passed new laws in February 2021 to restrict police access to TraceTogether data to only seven specific categories of serious crimes. Importantly, it made explicit reference to the importance of upholding public trust in leaders and its commitment to do so.

In the context of decision-making under rapid changes, uncertainty, incomplete information and new revelations,

BOX 2: (*Continued*)

the public has legitimate queries and trust concerns. Some of these issues and concerns have been addressed. However, the extent to which the public find the explanations and safeguards satisfactory will vary across individuals, depending on how they view the Government's account.

Some may be experiencing what I have called "trust-in-transition". This is a transition period in which the trustor (the individual member of the public) has feelings of doubt and ambivalence towards the trustee (the Government). It is a critical period because what occurs during this time can be highly impactful and "tilts" the trustor towards trust or distrust.

During trust-in-transition, the trustor experiences conflicting thoughts and mixed emotions. This occurs because the trustor had a previously positive perception of the trustee but is now undergoing negative experiences related to competence, integrity, benevolence or some combination of these dimensions.

Whether people move out of their transition into trust or distrust will depend on their belief in the Government's competence, integrity, and benevolence. They need to see that the Government can put citizen interests and well-being as the top priority and have the intention and sincerity to do so.

This public perception needs to be continuously earned by the government — it does not come automatically just because it existed previously.

BOX 3: STRATEGIC APPROACHES TO DEVELOP TRUST

There are strategic approaches to address trust issues and build trust. Here are four pairs of Ps to do so:

- **Be principled and pragmatic**
  Have a set of shared values and core guiding principles, while at the same time focusing on what is most or more critical in the practical situation.

- **Focus on prevention and promotion**
  Anticipate and be prepared to prevent negative outcomes from occurring while also aspiring and pursuing opportunities to bring about positive outcomes.

- **Have a pluralistic and paradoxical mindset**
  Take a wider range of different perspectives into account, and do not always seeing difficult decisions as zero-sum trade-off situations but instead consider how two seemingly contradictory goals may in fact be complementary.

- **Practise people-centricity and perspective-taking**
  Understand how people think, feel and act by appreciating people's expectations, evaluations and experiences and learn to see things from the other person's perspective.

ADDRESS PUBLIC TRUST

Addressing public trust is critical. High trust is necessary for leaders in business, non-profit organisations and especially government. They need to facilitate people to make good decisions, engage in positive behaviours, and work together to emerge stronger and better as individuals and as a society.

As we have seen, trust is neither random nor predetermined. Trust levels can be predicted to some extent, and they can be enhanced. We need to go beyond the trust score at any one point in time and see that trust is a process, and there could be transitions.

To understand trust, we need to appreciate its fragility and power. That means understanding the science of trust and translating it into practice to deal with trust erosion, trust repair and trust development.

www.ingramcontent.com/pod-product-compliance
Lightning Source LLC
Chambersburg PA
CBHW071951260326
41914CB00004B/795